MW01174384

To

_____

From

_____

Date

_____

TAKE
CHARGE,
RULE YOUR
WORLD

Discovering and Maximizing Your Authority
Over the Heavens, Earth and Sea

JOSHUA AMZAT

Take Charge, Rule Your World

Discovering and Maximizing Your Authority Over the Heavens, Earth and Sea

Copyright © 2018 by **Joshua Amzat**

ISBN: 978-1-944652-59-3

Published by:
Cornerstone Publishing
A Division of Cornerstone Creativity Group LLC
Info@thecornerstonepublishers.com
www.thecornerstonepublishers.com
516.547.4999

Author's Contact

For booking to speak at your next event or to order bulk copies of this book please use information below:

Email: joshuaamzat@hotmail.com
Phone number: +1 (832) 208-1069
www.jamzatdreamalive.com

DEDICATION

To the Holy Spirit, my Senior Partner.

To my wonderful and Godsend wife, Jane Amzat.

And to my two children, Princess Praise and Prince Joshua Amzat (Jnr.) whom I consider great blessings to their generation.

ACKNOWLEDGMENTS

I give foremost thanks to my heavenly Father, for the inspiration given to me to be able to write this book.

To my beloved and beautiful wife of over 12 years, Jane Amzat, I say a big "thank you", for standing by me and believing in me when nobody else did. Thanks for your numerous pressure to get this done and your words of wisdom. Your attention to family details has been valuable to me in my endeavors, and especially to complete this assignment given to me by God. I love you, Baby Jane.

To my daughter, Princess Praise, and my son, Prince Joshua Amzat (Jnr.), thanks for your love and support.

I thank all my friends and co-laborers in the ministry, who encouraged me when most needed. I am particularly grateful to the entire leadership and members of World Prayer Ministries and also Dunamis World Outreach. I appreciate your support over the years till now.

Thanks to the many writers, intellectuals and teachers of all hues from whom I have learned and thereby been enlightened.

Special thanks to my publisher, Pastor Gbenga Showunmi (Pastor Show) and the publication team for their exhibition of unbeatable publication skills throughout the process of putting this book together.

Thanks and God bless you all. I am grateful.

Pastor Joshua Amzat
Houston Texas, USA

CONTENTS

PART THREE: TAKE CHARGE, RULE THE HEAVENS

INTRODUCTION

In their 1994 album titled "I know Who Holds Tomorrow", Alison Kraus and the Cox Family included a particularly striking track, which they called, "Remind Me, Dear Lord". And true to the words of the song, if there is a time that believers need to be reminded of their true identity, position, power and authority on earth, now is that time. If there is a time that believers need to be reminded that being children of God, they themselves are gods, who are expected to reign on earth in full dominion as God reigns supreme in heaven, then the appropriate time is now.

I said this because contrary to the wonderful purpose of God for our redemption and the abundant provisions He has made for our dominion, what we see in the lives of many believers and in many congregations today are telltale signs of defeat, despair and despondency. Crises and conflicts, oppressions and afflictions, scandals and backslidings prevail in the lives of many church-goers, while Christianity itself is increasingly becoming an endangered way of life in many parts of the world.

Meanwhile, the ungodly and the agents of Satan are having a field day, recording unbelievable achievements in all spheres of life, introducing all sorts of inventions into the world, and wielding so much influence on the patterns of education, government, media, policy-making and so on in our communities and nations – much to our detriment. Essentially, children of God whose Father owns the universe are being boxed into a corner while the godless continue to have their way and even sometimes using the resources that should be ours against us.

What's the cause of this anomaly? Our laxity. Both individual believers and the church as a whole have been too laid back with regard to our understanding of the wonders of our world and the preeminent role that God has given us to play in it as humans and, more importantly, as partakers of the divine nature. We have largely been passive, with many of us thinking that we have nothing to do with the earth, since heaven is our ultimate home. And so the heathen get so emboldened to not only lay claim to the influence and dominion we should be having, but they even go as far as encroaching into the church with destructive influences.

This is exactly why the Holy Spirit has inspired this book to be written at this time. Believers everywhere need to be awakened to the reality of our authority over the universe and how far we have ceded it to Satan and his children. Someone once said: "The fall of man subjected the earth to the same corruption as the hearts of man, but the work Jesus did on the cross set the course for the reversal of this process and the return to our intended mandate. Instead, we as Christians tend to sit back while those who do not know the Lord cultivate and dominate the earth. This is not wrong. They are in fact doing what they were created to do, but they are doing it under a different master. Consider what the world would look like if we took up our God-given mandate and released, by restoration, the glory of creation to a watching world!"

This is a key reflection that the Lord wants us to make as we explore the contents of this book. The universe was made by God for His children, not by Satan for his agents. It is time for the individual believers and the church to awake out of slumber and begin to unearth the wonders, riches and possibilities that God has deposited in the universe for our benefit. This powerful discovery will certainly propel every believer to reclaim the dominion that God has given to us and to enjoy the immeasurable blessings that come with it.

PART 1

TAKE CHARGE, RULE THE EARTH

CHAPTER ONE

THE CONQUERING LIFE: A PERSONAL EXPERIENCE

In writing a book of this nature, I consider it necessary to begin with some background on my life as a Christian and a minister of God. This, I believe, will easily explain how I was privileged to come about the uncommon revelations in it.

I was born into a Muslim family and my grandfather was one of the frontrunners of Islam in our village in Ogun State, western Nigeria. He was a *khalifa*, a respected Islamic scholar and cleric, and was in fact, the head of all the Muslims in the village.

In those days (as it still is in some communities) it was an abomination to say you converted to Christianity. You would be cut off from the family. My father was very zealous with his faith. He often woke up earlier than most other Muslims to pray. He woke up as early as 3 o'clock every morning so as to spend some extra time praying. And he would go on to adhere to other prayer times in the day. Prayer thus became a natural activity for me as I was introduced to praying five times a day and fasting in the Ramadan period. Prayer became unconsciously etched in my psyche. This strict adherence to prayer times would help me maintain a disciplined prayer life when I eventually became a Christian.

I began to learn Arabic at a very young age, with the intention of becoming an Alfa. I had no idea that my desire for a close relationship with God was being channeled the wrong way. I continued this way until 1985, when my cousin introduced me to one of their Christian Union gatherings at Clerg Girls High School, Surulere. That was my first time of being in a Christian gathering. The minister there asked those who wanted to give their lives to Christ to indicate, and I did. A hand was laid upon me and I began to speak in tongues. However, since I came from another religious background, I did not really understand the significance of what had happened. I was zealous for the Lord for about four years but I soon started to become lukewarm.

A PECULIAR ENCOUNTER

On December 31st 1997, I was at a church service in Maryland, United States. The Pastor preaching that night seemed to be talking directly about me. That night, I had an encounter and I just knew that if I did not fully rededicate my life to God, I would die the next year. This might not make much sense to you but I had the strong witness in my spirit that something horrible would happen to me from that night on into the New Year.

I returned to London from that trip a changed person. I began to read my Bible for about 10 hours a day. Mind you, I had already set myself for full-time ministry, without knowing anything about the future. Soon after, I came in contact with Benny Hinn's book, (Good morning Holy Spirit). That book changed my life. I read how Benny used to pray for 10 hours and I wondered how that was possible. I was so challenged that I asked my brother that we should give it a try. However, after one hour of trying, we were already exhausted and didn't know what else to pray about again.

I guess the Holy Spirit who saw our hearts, knew that our yearning was not for self-gratification. So, He stepped in for us. I remember often locking myself in the room and asking the Holy Spirit to teach me how to pray. Soon, I began to pray for up to 14 hours without even knowing the details of my future ministerial assignment. In a way, my inadequacy in expressing myself in words also helped me to derive joy in taking solace in the Holy Spirit. Because people did not really understand me when I spoke, I had become insecure as a youth. This insecurity drew me closer to the Holy Spirit. I often cried my heart out to the Lord, because only in the place of prayer did I have full assurance that somebody listened to and understood me.

My Christian life has been a life of prayer. The strict prayer routine of my Islamic background could have contributed to this. I have always wanted to do more and be more, without leaving any room for complacency.

HELP FOR MY WEAKNESS

The Holy Spirit has been of tremendous help to me throughout the course of my Christian journey (Romans 8:26). He helped me as a bachelor to flee youthful lusts, as instructed in 2 Timothy 2:22. Joseph had to flee from Potiphar's wife, even when the Bible had not yet been compiled. What kept him? The Holy Spirit, through his dedication to God. Joseph knew where he was going, so he did not allow the pleasure of Potiphar's house to rob him of his destiny. My prayer today is that God will help you to abstain from every ungodly desire.

Indeed, whether single or married, it is impossible to have a victorious walk as a believer without a fervent prayer life. This is why the enemy is fighting against prayers in the body of Christ. He knows that if we cannot pray, our ability to abstain from sin and obtain all-round dominion will be less likely.

Moreover, the place of prayer in birthing miracles cannot be denied. Most of the miracles I have seen in our ministry were birthed in the place of prayer. There was the case of a woman who had been such a blessing to the ministry. A day before Thanksgiving celebration in 2012, the enemies struck her with aneurysm and an enlarged heart. We were told that she died for 30 minutes at Memorial Hermann Hospital before she came back to life. Like Jacob (in Genesis 32:24-28), I remember telling my family to go and visit one of our family friends on Thanksgiving Day. Thereafter, I began to plead with God. After spending close to 10 hours interceding with my face to the ground, news came that she had started responding to treatment and soon got better. Glory be to God!

Regarding the life of Jacob, the power of prayer is particularly noteworthy. He had to wrestle with his past in the place of prayers. It was in the place of encounter that God changed his name to Israel, which, according to the angel with whom he wrestled, signifies that

> *"As a prince hast thou power with God and with men, and hast prevailed" (verse 28, KJV).*

No wonder when he met Esau, whom he had wronged many years before, Esau could no longer revenge because it was Israel he met, as Jacob had died in the place of encounter with God. It was Jacob that offended Esau and not Israel. In the place of prayer, power is birthed and lives are transformed.

THE MINISTRY OF PRAYER

From the time of the Early Church, the ministry of prayer has been the mark of the high calling of true believers. This is the secret of many great believers' power. God wants to help mankind; yet God mostly does not do anything in the earthly realm without prayers being offered.

This is why in Acts 6:4, the apostle says "...we will give ourselves continually to prayer and to the ministry of the word." Here, the apostle uses an expression which means giving such marked attention and such deep concern to an activity that it becomes the ruling passion of one's life. The key word here is "continually". In other words, the early apostles believed and advocated that the life of a believer must continually be a life of intense prayer. This does not necessarily mean that believers must be on their knees every time; rather it means that at every moment, our spirit must be in communion with the Spirit of God.

That said, it still must be emphasized that anyone called into the ministry of prayer must spend hours in the closet, burdened by need which the Holy Spirit puts in their spirit, until the result comes. You are never wearied until you see the desire of the heavenly Father manifest.

My prayer for you is that you will be a believer with a few words before man but many words before God in the closet. It is written of Jesus Christ, our perfect example, that He

> *"offered up prayers and supplications, with vehement cries and tears to Him who was able to save Him from death, and was heard because of His godly fear" (Hebrews 5:7).*

Christ offered prayers and supplication with strong crying and shedding of tears unto God – which shows the fervency of His prayer life. But not only was His prayer life fervent, it was also frequent, consistent and spontaneous. He prayed in the day (Mark 1:35) and in the night. Sometimes He prayed all night long, simply to know and do the will of the Father (Luke 6:12).

I have to also emphasize that for the ministry of prayer to be effective, we have to rely on the Holy Spirit, who is the believer's Comforter, Advocate, and the Spirit of intercession (Romans 8:26-27). We need Him to purge us of every worldly desire and fill us with heavenly desires. We need Him to take away all manifestations of self-will from us and ensure that the will of God is fully manifested and perfected in our lives, churches and communities.

BOOK THRUST: MAKE YOUR LIFE COUNT!

Let me make it clear from the outset: The essence of delving into such profound revelations as you will find throughout this book is to trigger a phenomenal change in your life, destiny and ministry. It is to place you at the pedestal of awareness that God intends you to be, to make you understand who God has created and called you to be, the potential you have as a human and as a believer, and above all, to rouse you into functioning in full dominion, with all the resources that God has placed at your disposal.

It bothers me, as I know it bothers God, to see many people, believers especially, living an inferior, ordinary, average or "typical" life - which is actually a defeated life (yes, with God, there's no room for averageness or mediocrity - you're either a victor or a victim; a failure or a success!). Put simply, if you're living below God's expectations for you and you have accepted it as the norm, then you have automatically consigned yourself to the valley of failure.

Let me quickly show you an apt illustration of the condition of most people on earth and the exact position that God wants you to be in revealing the truths in this book. The Scripture says in Genesis 36:22-24:

> "And the sons of Lotan were Hori and Hemam. Lotan's sister was Timna. These were the sons of Shobal: Alvan, Manahath, Ebal, Shepho, and Onam. These were the sons of Zibeon: both Ajah and Anah. This was the Anah who found the water in the wilderness as he pastured the donkeys of his father Zibeon."

Were you initially bored with the genealogical drift of the passage? I won't be surprised if you were. Most people are bored with genealogies and records, which is why many don't read scripture books like Leviticus, Numbers and Chronicles. However, as the Bible rightly says that every scripture is inspired of God and profitable (2 Timothy 3:16), you will find that hidden in the genealogies, numbers and records as you have in these books of the Bible are powerful secrets to understanding our faith and enjoying manifold blessings from God.

Am I digressing? No. That exposition on genealogy is indeed a summary of the message in this book and particularly the passage above which I will be exploring shortly. Here is the connection. As I mentioned before, many people are living just ordinary lives and many end up dying unfulfilled and without fulfilling their mandates on earth. Why this happens is that just like those who don't see anything special about genealogical books, many are limited in their understanding of the world around them. They are contented with simply admiring its beauties and lamenting its uncertainties. Yet, there's so much more that they can do about the universe, as we will soon consider.

Let's return to our passage in Genesis. If you observe closely, every other name in the verses above was mentioned casually or as a matter of necessity. The reason is that there was nothing significant about them, other than the fact that they were on earth at one time or the other. Yes, each of them had a record but their lives were so similar to each other in mediocrity that it was not considered necessary to delve into their lives without boring both the writer and the reader. However, on getting to Anah, there was a pause before moving to the next name. Why was this? The narrative of his life was not like the narrative of the lives of others. He made a huge impact and left an indelible footprint in his community by discovering something about the earth that those before him or around him had not discovered. In other words, his life was extraordinary because he achieved the seemingly unachievable.

WHAT'S THE POINT?

This book is not about the life of Anah, that's for sure. But there is something I want you to observe, which will form a basis for what God wants us to see here. Since we know that God inspired the writing of the Scripture, it means that if He deemed it fit that special attention should be given to the life of this man, then it should tell you that making your life count on earth is something that God places a high premium on. It is my prayer that your life will command attention in heaven and on earth.

What this implies for you is that you were not created to just survive or exist; you were created to have dominion over the earth - to be the instrument through which the glories, beauties, riches and possibilities implanted in the universe would be understood, discovered and exploited. You were not created to be a helpless conformist to the ups-and-downs of life; you were created to be a problem-solver, a pacesetter and a game-changer. You were created to make your life count!

CHAPTER TWO

WONDERS OF THE EARTH

Everything God made is glorious, and the earth is a brilliant reflection of this. Make no mistake about it – the earth, especially, the ground below us - is a treasure house of wonders, riches, mysteries and possibilities. Geologists and geophysicists who devote themselves to studying the composition, structure and other physical attributes of the earth have continued to be amazed at its various features, many of which have continued to defy understanding and explanation, even to the best of scientists.

Becky Oskin, a senior writer for *LifeScience*, wrote in 2014: "When the first Earth Day was held in 1970, geologists were still putting the finishing touches on plate tectonics, the model that explains how the Earth's surface takes shape. More than 40 years later, many riddles still remain when it comes to our planet." Corroborating this, another science researcher wrote, "Geology is full of strange mysteries, from towering structures to small formations. The more we examine these deceptively complicated phenomena, the less we understand their origins and the processes that created them."

Some of the earth's phenomena that have continued to baffle scientists include the core of the earth, which, despite all attempts, remains unreachable for humans. Scientists are also bewildered by the exact causes of earthquakes and how to prevent them. In fact, the biggest ever attempt made to forecast an earthquake was between 1985 and 1994, when scientists from the United States Geological Survey and the University of California, Berkeley, predicted (with a 90 to 95 percent confidence level) that there would be one at Parkfield, California, by 1994. In a bid to catch the coming temblor and minimize its impact, the scientists set an elaborate array of sophisticated equipment around Parkfield, starting in 1985.

Interestingly, however, no earthquake occurred within the specified period, leaving the scientists red-faced and even more baffled. It wasn't until ten years later in 2004 that an earthquake occurred in the area.

Yet, our concern here goes deeper than the physical features or geological complexities of the earth because part of what many scientists do not know is that the earth itself is not just a mere static geographical formation. Like most other natural and seemingly ordinary components of the universe, the earth has a life of its own which responds to the spiritual and demonstrates the supernatural. The scripture clearly enlightens us on this and it is one essential truth you need to grasp if you will make your life count, have absolute dominion and fulfill your destiny on earth.

Here are some crucial, scripture-based truths about the earth that should begin to make you rethink your understanding of the earth and then get you repositioned for unstoppable dominion.

1. Every creature has its origin in the earth.

Concerning animals, for instance, Genesis 2:19 says,

> *"And out of the ground the Lord God formed every beast of the field, and every fowl of the air..."*

This is the same with the creation of plants. Genesis 1:11-12 says,

> *"And God said, Let the earth bring forth grass, the herb yielding seed, and the fruit tree yielding fruit after his kind, whose seed is in itself, upon the earth: and it was so. And the earth brought forth grass, and herb yielding seed after his kind, and the tree yielding fruit, whose seed was in itself."*

Even man, who is the crown of God's creation and was made in the image and likeness of God, has his origin in the earth. Verse 7 of the same Genesis 2 says,

> *"And the Lord God formed man of the dust of the ground, and breathed into his nostrils the breath of life; and man became a living soul."*

Is it any wonder that all creatures return to dust eventually? For man in particular, God not only confirmed that his origin was the earth but also declared that he would eventually return to the earth, except for his spirit which will return to God (Genesis 3:19; Ecclesiastes 12:7).

2. The earth is man's heritage.

Yes, the earth belongs to you and to me. It is the inheritance of mankind bequeathed to him by God. Are you surprised? Don't be. I already told you that these are scriptural truths; so every point here is taken directly from the Scripture. Concerning the earth being the inheritance of man, Psalm 115:16 says,

> *"The heaven, even the heavens, are the Lord's; But the earth He has given to the children of men."*

Isn't this super awesome? God has given us the earth to take charge of it and customize it to our advantage. And I guess you can see better why I said that our focus in exploring the earth is to make us take our rightful place of dominion in it. It is to make us detest and reject anything that makes us live below the life that God has called us to live. If a property is willed to you, for example, would it not be abnormal for you to be living in the basement of the building? I am sure that you would take the best part of the apartment to yourself. So, it's time to reflect: if God is your Father and He has given you the earth, are you reigning on it, or are you just "managing" to get by?

3. God has placed hidden riches in different parts of the earth.

Not only has God given the earth to men, but, as a considerate and benevolent Father, He has also stocked (that is, LOADED) it inexhaustible riches and resources. Some of these resources are meant to sustain and enhance the quality of the life of man, while others are mean to enrich him. And what's more, God has promised that these riches will be given to His own children on earth. How privileged are you! Here's how He put it:

"I will give you the treasures of darkness. And hidden riches of secret places. That you may know that I, the Lord Who call you by your name, am the God of Israel." *(Isaiah 45:3).*

Note that the expressions "treasures of darkness" and "hidden riches of secret places" do not in any way connote anything questionable; they simply connote invisibility. In other words, while the earth is saturated with great riches and possibilities, not all of them are visible. In fact, most of the riches of the earth are either hidden deep beneath the surface of the earth (in form of mineral resources, petroleum, gas etc.) or they are hidden in creatures of the earth such as plants and animals.

Again, the riches are said to be "hidden" because, sometimes, to the physical eye, a land may appear to be totally barren, a plant may appear to be good for nothing, an animal may seem only fit for eating and nothing more; yet there could be myriads of benefits and discoveries that are waiting to be found and developed in them.

I have shown you from the Scripture how Anah found something remarkable enough to be recorded for generations in a place that was considered a wilderness. The Scripture also contains the example of Hagar, who saw a well of water in a place she had considered to be good for nothing else, other than being a suitable graveyard for her son, Ishmael. There is also the example of Isaac,

Take Charge, Rule Your World

who sowed and had a bountiful harvest in a land that was being ravaged by famine. We shall be paying detailed attention to these examples in a later chapter.

In our contemporary times, we have heard stories of people who made remarkable discoveries in seemingly unlikely places and sometimes from seemingly unlikely plants and animals. There is the inspiring case of George Washington Carver, who discovered hundreds of products from the peanuts, which until then had been considered good for nothing but to eat a little and feed livestock. There is also the popular story of "Acres of Diamonds", attributed to Russell H. Conwell, founder and first president of Temple University in Philadelphia. It is about a farmer who had sold his land to go search for diamonds, only for the buyer of the land to find a huge reserve of diamonds on the same land. I will provide details of these examples later on.

4. Earth was created to be fully inhabited, explored and exploited.

If every part of the earth is filled with fullness of treasures and resources, what is the purpose? Why would God, in creating the earth, bless it so richly? Here is the answer in Isaiah 45:18:

> *"For thus says the Lord, Who created the heavens, Who is God, Who formed the earth and made it, Who has established it, Who did not create it in vain, Who formed it to be inhabited...".*

Two amazing facts stand out in this passage. First, the earth is not an accidental creation (certainly, not from any "Big Bang", as some scientists would have us believe). God

Himself formed it and enriched it. And since all His works are known to Him from the beginning, He already knew which nation or people that would inhabit every part of the earth and had thus deposited necessary riches and resources in their portion of the earth.

The second fact is that no part of the earth was created in vain; nor is any of the earth's beauties or riches just meant for show. God created the earth to be inhabited and its infinite resources and capabilities to be discovered and enjoyed. Beyond that, abundance of mysteries and riches abound within the surface of the earth, which God wants mankind to explore and exploit to our own advantage.

Note that to explore is to search and discover. But to exploit is to maximize what has been discovered and put it into profitable use. This is why you will find that almost every vocation in the world has to do with studying the earth and its inhabitants, exploring the resources of the earth (including plants and animals), putting these resources (or raw materials) into profitable use, or merchandizing the direct or indirect products of the earth. There is an even more amazing implication to this which I will be showing you in the next point.

5. Earth is enriched with all that its creatures need for sustenance and survival.

This is really remarkable and I want you to pay particular attention. All that is needed for the nourishment, health, rejuvenation and healing for all the creatures that emerged from the earth have been infused into the same earth and its products. Of course, my ultimate focus here is humans, but let me first generalize the point to all of earth's creatures, so you can get a clear and challenging revelation here. Since the earth was carefully formed by God, He has ensured that all the creatures that would inhabit it had more than enough to sustain them, regardless of how many they may be. This is why the Scripture refers to the fatness of the earth (Genesis 27:28).

In understanding this truth, we need to return to the account of the creation and discover God's awesome purpose for the earth and its inhabitants. Recall that the first thing that God called into existence was light. Thereafter, He commanded the waters under the heavens to be gathered, so that dry land could appear. After this, God called forth plants, herbs and trees and commanded them to yield fruits. It was after this that He made the lower and higher animals, and ultimately He made man.

Has it ever occurred to you why God had to follow this sequence? It's a simple logic which should make you understand that our God is a strategic planner who would never create any life without the means for it to be sustained. Plants need both the nourishment of the earth, as well as light, to survive. God ensured that these were provided before plants were created. Lower animals mostly need plants for nourishment, while higher animals need mostly the lower animals and plants for survival. Humans, being omnivorous beings, need all the previously created creatures for sustenance and health.

Now, this is where I'm going. Neither plants nor animals in their natural habitats ever have to struggle to feed from the earth. Even without any knowledge of agriculture, animal husbandry, manufacturing or merchandizing, every other creature gets its daily meals from the earth. These include the birds of the sky who also have to look to the earth to survive, and they have their fill daily. In fact, in pointing out the pointlessness of worrying about daily meals for humans, Christ had to use the example of the birds of the air:

> *"Therefore I say to you, do not worry about your life, what you will eat or what you will drink; nor about your body, what you will put on. Is not life more than food and the body more than clothing? Look at the birds of the air, for they neither sow nor reap nor gather into barns; yet your heavenly Father feeds them. Are you not of more value than they?" (Matthew 6:25-31).*

So, if the birds of the air and other creatures, who neither sow nor reap, could have their needs met from the earth, due to the provisions that God makes for them, why should you as a human not have your needs met? It is an aberration of the most absurd proportion. All you need to survive and succeed is right here. Simply ask God to open your eyes!

The deeper implication of this is that there is really no reason why anyone on earth should live in poverty and want, or lack a vocation. As long as man can know what to do with the earth, then he will continue to find its yield inestimable and inexhaustible. That is a cardinal reason for creating man in the first place. God's purpose was not for man to just observe the earth; His purpose was for man to "till" it (Genesis 2:5).

The dictionary defines tilling as "working" or "ploughing". To summarize this, it means you should take charge of the earth by working, commanding it and making it work in your favor. All these will be explored in detail in the subsequent chapters. But for now, establish it in your mind that God's purpose is for your life to count while on earth. He has created so much for you to discover, to exploit and to enjoy. And every productive activity you engage in, including every new breakthrough you make on earth, continues to gladden His heart because that's His original purpose for you.

6. The earth can hear, execute commands and keep records.

I mentioned earlier that the earth has a life of its own. And like all living things, it can hear and can reproduce (that is, bring forth) according as it is commanded. God, who created the earth, surely knows about these capabilities. This was why He spoke to the earth during the creation process:

> *"Then God said, "Let the earth bring forth grass, the herb that yields seed, and the fruit tree that yields fruit according to its kind, whose seed is in itself, on the earth"; and it was so. And the earth brought forth grass, the herb that yields seed according to its kind, and the tree that yields fruit, whose seed is in itself according to its kind. And God saw that it was good." Genesis 1: 12-13.*

Did you observe that not only did the earth hear and respond to God's command, but brought forth exactly what God ordered it to? And guess what? What it brought forth was GOOD! My prayer is that the earth will perpetually produce that which is good for you. But you must also take it upon yourself to declare what you want while you are on the earth. God declared what He wanted from the earth, and the earth gave it to Him. The question is: What do YOU want from the earth? You just must learn to proclaim and declare the kind of life you want to live on earth.

Interestingly, it wasn't only God that spoke to the earth. Prophets of old too understood that the earth indeed has a personality that can be communicated with. For instance, Moses, in admonishing the children of Israel on the need to devote themselves to serving the Lord all their lives, as well as the dangers of forsaking Him, had to repeatedly call the earth to witness the solemn declarations he was making to them (See Deuteronomy 4:26; 30:19). Again, in chapter 32 of the same Deuteronomy, Moses again called the earth to witness as he gave his farewell address to the Israelites.

> *"Give ear, O heavens, and I will speak, and let the earth hear the words of my mouth."* (Genesis 32:1).

Isaiah also did a similar thing in Isaiah 1:2, *"Hear, O heavens, and give ear, O earth: for the Lord hath spoken, I have nourished and brought up children, and they have rebelled against me."*

Why should the earth continually be called upon to witness, if it is as lifeless as many of us think?

Jeremiah even went beyond showing us that the earth can hear; he showed us that the earth can record and execute what it hears! Jeremiah 22:29-30 (KJV) says,

> *"O earth, earth, earth, hear the word of the Lord. Thus*

saith the Lord, Write ye this man childless, a man that shall not prosper in his days: for no man of his seed shall prosper, sitting upon the throne of David, and ruling any more in Judah."

The earth here is being charged with the responsibility of ensuring that Jeconiah (also known as Coniah, Jehoiachin or Jechonias), who was then king of Judah, was to be a failure and must be accounted to be childless. In other words, as the latter parts of the verse shows, even though he already had offspring, none of them would prosper or ever become a king again in the land. And of course, the earth did as it was told. Just a few months of his reign, he and his household and thousands of other Jews were exiled into Babylon. And, again, none of his seven children ever became a king in the land, even after their return from captivity.

We also find that in the New Testament Jesus spoke to a product of the earth, a fig tree, and the earth swung into action to execute the command. Mark 11:12-14, 20 narrates:

"Now the next day, when they had come out from Bethany, He was hungry. And seeing from afar a fig tree having leaves, He went to see if perhaps He would find something on it. When He came to it, He found nothing but leaves, for it was not the season for figs. In response Jesus said to it, "Let no one eat fruit from you ever again...Now in the morning, as they passed by, they saw the fig tree dried up from the roots."

The earth responded to Christ's declaration here by ensuring that the tree was killed through deprivation of oxygen and decimation of the pH of the soil. Even though the tree was symbolic and Christ's declaration prophetic, it gives us a clear insight into a powerful possibility of the earth in stifling and killing everything that constitutes an obstacle to the people of God or the work of God.

I believe one major truth that God wants to reveal to us in making us know that the earth can hear is that our utterances must be guarded at all times. Our words are like seeds and the earth being able to hear and reproduce will bring forth for us, whatsoever seed it picks from us. Death and life are in the power of the tongue and they that love it shall eat of the fruit (Proverbs 18:21).

7. The earth abhors bloodshed.

One of the ways that the earth keeps records is to ensure that no innocent blood spilt on it goes unaccounted for. The soul of man is precious to God and any act of bloodshed committed, either through abortion, slander or outright murder, does not escape the notice of the earth, to which all flesh returns. Isaiah 26:21 says,

> *"For behold, the Lord comes out of His place to punish the inhabitants of the earth for their iniquity; the earth will also disclose her blood, And will no more cover her slain."*

We find examples of what the earth does about murder in different [arts of the Bible. God declared to Cain that the blood of Abel, his brother, who he had murdered continued to cry out from the earth for justice (Genesis 4:9-10). Consequently, Cain received a curse from the Lord in recompense. Also, when David plotted the killing of Uriah, Bathsheba's husband, because he wanted the wife, the blood of Uriah kept crying for vengeance. Thus, God sent

Nathan the prophet to David to pronounce the judgment of God upon David's household. Nathan declared

> *"Now therefore, the sword shall never depart from your house, because you have despised Me, and have taken the wife of Uriah the Hittite to be your wife.'*
>
> *Thus says the Lord: 'Behold, I will raise up adversity against you from your own house; and I will take your wives before your eyes and give them to your neighbor, and he shall lie with your wives in the sight of this sun… because by this deed you have given great occasion to the enemies of the Lord to blaspheme, the child also who is born to you shall surely die" (2 Samuel 12:10-14).*

You must have noticed that even though it was David that shed the blood of Uriah, the judgment for the evil deed was placed upon his entire household. Even the innocent baby that was born from the illicit affair with Bathsheba was not spared. What this means is that judgment for spilling blood on earth is very severe, because the earth will continue to cry out until appropriate judgment is meted out.

The wider implication of this is that the reason some people continue to face afflictions, oppressions and all forms of hardship in their lives could be because of the blood of the innocent that had been shed by their forefathers. Especially in communities and continents like Africa, where human sacrifices and other forms of wanton killings had been carried out against the innocents (such as twins) in the past, crises, conflicts and retrogressions are often the resultant consequences. And except there is acknowledgment and repentance, the effects may continue to reverberate from generation to generation. That is how serious the aftermath of bloodshed can be on the earth.

Christ also confirms the certainty of accountability for bloodshed in his condemnation of the scribes and the Pharisees in Matthew 23:34-35:

> *"Wherefore, behold, I send unto you prophets, and wise men, and scribes: and some of them ye shall kill and crucify; and some of them shall ye scourge in your synagogues, and persecute them from city to city: That upon you may come all the righteous blood shed upon the earth, from the blood of righteous Abel unto the blood of Zacharias son of Barachias, whom ye slew between the temple and the altar."*

You may have noticed that when water is poured on the ground, it goes into it instantly. However, when blood is shed on the ground, the ground keeps it on its surface. If it's hard for the earth to cover up blood in the natural, then you can understand why, as long as the earth remains, no murder case can go without leaving a trace. The earth will always cry out for vengeance.

What this calls for is utmost caution on the part of every believer, so that no innocent blood is shed because of our negligence or outright scheming.

Jesus Christ again demonstrated the powers of the earth in recording and witnessing against an individual or community when He told the disciples:

> *"And whosoever shall not receive you, nor hear your words, when ye depart out of that house or city, shake off the dust of your feet. Verily I say unto you, It shall*

41

> *be more tolerable for the land of Sodom and Gomorrah in the day of judgment, than for that city" (Matthew 10:14-15).*

Jesus gave this instruction because there is a powerful connection between the dust of the earth and the feet of mankind. Contact between the ground and the feet establishes some sort of covenant that connects the individual to every portion of the ground where his feet touch. This is why God told Joshua that wherever the soles of his feet shall tread upon will be given to him as an inheritance (Joshua 1:3). Jesus, therefore, in telling the disciples to shake off the dust of their feet meant that they totally disconnect themselves from such communities and leave them to their certain destruction.

Like many other issues that have to with the mysteries of the universe, the example I gave about the connection between the feet and the ground may seem strange. But I can tell you categorically that this is a proven reality. In my younger years as a Muslim, one day, my father went to a spiritualist to seek help over his business. The spiritualist told him to bring the sand from the Friday prayer gathering which was always well-attended. The logic was that, as people thronged the prayer ground, so would they flock to my father to patronize his business. And the magic seemed to work. This was in the 1980s and it remained a mystery because the earth responded to the spiritual authority of the priest who was not even a believer.

I have also heard of people using the sand from other people's feet for diabolical reasons and they always seem to get their expected result. I am neither a believer in nor a supporter of magic in any way. However I have brought up the illustrations to show you how much of our authority on earth we're abandoning to the heathen.

8. The earth has a mouth that can open up to devour.

This is another wonder of the earth that the saints of old were aware of but which many believers today seem to ignore. The earth has a mouth that can devour any of its inhabitants when necessary. When Korah, Dathan, and Abiram rebelled against Moses and challenged his authority in the wilderness, Moses did not argue with them. Instead, he spoke to the earth to settle the matter.

"And Moses said, Hereby ye shall know that the Lord hath sent me to do all these works; for I have not done them of mine own mind. If these men die the common death of all men, or if they be visited after the visitation of all men; then the Lord hath not sent me. But if the Lord make a new thing, and the earth open her mouth, and swallow them up, with all that appertain unto them, and they go down quick into the pit; then ye shall understand that these men have provoked the Lord. And it came to pass, as he had made an end of speaking all these words, that the ground clave asunder that was under them: And the earth opened her mouth, and swallowed them up, and their houses, and all the men that appertained unto Korah, and all their goods. They, and all that appertained to them, went down alive into the pit, and the earth closed upon them: and they perished from among the congregation. And all Israel that were round about them fled at the cry of them: for they said, Lest the earth swallow us up also." Numbers 16:28-34.

Yes, indeed, the adversaries of the people of God will tremble in fear, when they know that we have such authority over the earth to summon it to our aid when necessary. Settle it in your mind from today – the earth can open its mouth to swallow up your enemies. I see your enemies being swallowed up in Jesus' name.

Let me repeat, for emphasis, as believers, God has given us the authority to command the earth to open up and swallow our enemies. The question however is, how often do we exercise this authority? Sadly, it is the devil and his agents who understand the potential of the earth to devour that are using it against the people of God. It is a reality of life that anything God does, the enemy will always want to do the counterfeit. As I write now, the glories, destinies and blessings of many believers have been swallowed by the earth through the activities of the evil ones. It is your duty therefore to command the earth to spit out your testimonies, breakthrough and all that belongs to you. My prayer for you is that everything that pertains to you that has been buried by the enemy will be resurrected in Jesus' name.

Even more worrisome is that, for some people, they themselves have been buried in the spiritual realm – meaning that they are just walking corpses. And it is for this reason that they are not able to achieve anything meaningful in life or live a life of purpose. Still, the promise of God for such, as they read and apply the principles in this book is:

"Behold, O My people, I will open your graves and cause you to come up from your graves..." (Ezekiel 37:12).

He is faithful who has promised and He will certainly make good His promise.

9. The earth can help the people of God.

The earth can be of tremendous help to anyone that knows how to command it. Specifically for the people of God, the earth can help them in two ways. One is to act as a form of defense against the attack of the evil ones; the second is to help fight against their enemies. We find a good example of the earth rising to the defense of a child of God in Revelation 12:15-16,

> *"So the serpent spewed water out of his mouth like a flood after the woman, that he might cause her to be carried away by the flood. But the earth helped the woman, and the earth opened its mouth and swallowed up the flood which the dragon had spewed out of his mouth."*

What a remarkable privilege we have as children of God! The Lord has declared that no weapon fashioned against us shall prosper (Isaiah 54:17). And one of the ways that the Lord frustrates the plots, conspiracies and devices of the wicked against the children of God and against the church of God is to cause the earth to swallow them up through our authority.

As for the earth rising to the help of the people of God in fighting against their enemies, I have shown you an example earlier on how the earth opened its mouth to consume the adversaries of Moses. Of course, to some people, it's all a myth that is too good to be true; yet I have read about how some men in the part of Africa where I come from were swallowed up by the earth. These are real life experiences. And I tell you that if it has happened before, it can happen again.

We also find an example of the earth being used as a weapon against the enemies of the people of God in Exodus 8:16-19, "So the Lord said to Moses, *"Say to Aaron, 'Stretch out your rod, and strike the dust of the land, so that it may become lice throughout all the land of Egypt".* And they did so. For Aaron stretched out his hand with his rod and struck the dust of the earth, and it became lice on man and beast. All the dust of the land became lice throughout all the land of Egypt. Now the magicians so worked with their enchantments to bring forth lice, but they could not. So there were lice on man and beast. Then the magicians said to Pharaoh, "This is the finger of God."

Isn't it time we begin to show the adversaries of the people of God – including the most skeptical of them – that there is indeed something called the finger of God that could be fierce and terrible against all who oppose His will? The earth is at our disposal, and at our command, it can make life unbearable for all who, like Pharaoh and the Egyptians, stubbornly insist on standing in the way of the people of God or the church of God, through their words, actions and policies.

10. The earth has habitations of cruelty

Well, it is an unpleasant reality, but it is one we have to learn to deal with because we have the authority to do so. Psalm 74:20 says,

> *"Have respect unto the covenant: for the dark places of the earth are full of the habitations of cruelty." (KJV)*

46

Contrary to the view of many believers, the earth is not a playground; it is a battlefield that is FULL of the habitations of cruelty. The psalmist, like many believers in Bible days, was aware of this and it is for our good that we bear this in mind as we go about our daily activities. It is this awareness that will keep us vigilant and triumphant in our Christian warfare. Paul the Apostle says in 2 Corinthians 2:11,

> *"Lest Satan should take advantage of us; for we are not ignorant of his devices."*

1 John 5:18 further reveals to us that we are not alone in affirming our authority over the earth; the devil and his demons too want to have full control. It says,

> *"We know that we are of God, and the whole world lies under the sway of the wicked one."*

The sway of the wicked one pervades the entire earth and manifests in all the cruelties, wickedness, savagery and wanton destructions that we witness from day to day.

The origins of the habitations of cruelty in the earth should not surprise you. Revelation 12:12 says,

> *"...Woe to the inhabitants of the earth and the sea! For the devil has come down to you, having great wrath, because he knows that he has a short time."*

Having been conquered and flung from heaven, it is natural for the devil and his legion of fallen angels to vent their fury on the earth and the inhabitants – the ultimate aim of which is to frustrate God's purpose in creating the earth and putting man in charge of it.

I sincerely hope that your heart is being stirred within you, reader, as you observe the revelations in the various scriptural references that we have considered. Within them, you will find a major difference between the believers of old and those of us in "modern" times - especially why those in Bible days seemed able to experience spectacular miracles which many of us in the church rarely experience these days. Besides, because these people of old knew how to use their authority over the earth, it brought the fear of God upon the heathen and they acknowledged His supremacy. It is because many believers have become so scientific in our thinking and thus unable to demonstrate earth-moving faith that many unbelievers continue to have a field day, wreaking all sorts of havocs and making all sorts of ungodly claims. My prayer is that the Lord will rouse us up in Jesus' name.

CHAPTER THREE

A MANDATE WITH A BLESSING

Near the end of his life, Jean-Paul Sartre, the renowned French philosopher, declared to a friend of his: "I do not feel that I am the product of chance, a speck of dust in the universe, but someone who was expected, prepared, prefigured. In short, a being whom only a Creator could put here; and this idea of a creating hand refers to God."

Although Sartre came to this understanding almost too late, that observation of his is worth pondering on, as it tallies with the uniform testimony of the Scripture concerning the creation of man. Indeed, we have a remarkable revelation in Genesis 1:26 that ought to make us re-evaluate the essence of our existence on earth and the extent to which we are justifying our purpose. Just after God had created the earth and imbued it with all the amazing wonders and possibilities that we have considered in the previous chapter, something happened.

"Then God said, "Let Us make man in Our image, according to Our likeness; let them have dominion... over all the earth..." (Genesis 1:26).

Here, we have it clearly stated that man was not a creature of divine whim; he was a creature that was truly "expected, prepared and prefigured." He was the pinnacle of God's creation and everything about his creation reflects this. His creation included a special introduction, with emphasis on the collaborative work of the Trinity that must be involved. Not only that, the specification of his creation – which is a special one - is repeated, as if for emphasis. And most importantly, it was after man had been created that God considered all He had made to be "very good", as opposed to just good.

Summarizing this distinctive attention given to man in the creation, Louis Berkhof, the influential theologian, stated: "According to Scripture the essence of man consists in this, that he is the image of God. As such he is distinguished from all other creatures and stands supreme as the head and crown of the entire creation."

JUSTIFICATION OF THE MANDATE

So, what was the purpose of the careful thought, attention and details that went into the creation of man? As the same Genesis 1:26 shows, not only was man's unique specification given, but the purpose of the special specification was equally stated. In other words, there is a reason that man, unlike other creatures of the earth was not called forth from the earth; there is a reason that God had to "make" (that is, form) him in His own image and likeness – he is not only to have the nature of God but to exercise God's dominion over the earth. He is not to be subject to the earth but to subject the earth to himself. R.C. Sproul has rightly stated: "We go back to creation and we see that man is made in the image and in the likeness of God, not in the sense that God has a body, but in terms of our nature. You are called to be living images that reflect and communicate the character of God Himself."

There was no way that man could have had dominion over what had produced him. Put differently, if man had been entirely from the earth like all other creatures, then he should have perpetually been a subject of the dictates of the earth; he shouldn't have been able to exercise power to exploit, transform, manage or customize the earth. So, this distinction in our creation contains a powerful message that must constantly resonate in our minds, as humans and especially as believers. As John McArthur states, "The truth that humanity was made in the likeness of God is the starting point for a biblical understanding of the nature of man…It reveals the very essence of the meaning and purpose of human life. It is full of practical and doctrinal significance."

A key part of the practical and doctrinal significance of God creating man in His image and likeness is that man is essentially created to function like God on the earth. He was endowed with God-like attributes so he can be God's active representative on earth, especially as he has been given the earth to manage. Daniel Becker in one his writings aptly noted, ""Imago Dei" is Latin for the "image of God." To be created imago Dei means being endowed with an immortal spirit, a capacity to know and be known by God, a measure of autonomy and free will in the areas of thought and action, each of which separates us from the rest of creation."

The deeper implication of this is that since God began to work on the earth from the time when it was totally void, calling forth those things that be not as though they were, then we must continue the responsibility of configuring and transfiguring the earth to our advantage and ultimately to the glory of God. God Himself demonstrated that He had given man power to have dominion over the governance the earth by bringing the creatures of the earth to him to name and classify. And the Scripture notes that whatever Adam called each animal remained its permanent name. God made it clear to Adam and by extension to us that the earth and its riches, resources, mysteries and potentials are ours to maximize. How much of this mandate are we fulfilling?

CONSTANCY OF THE MANDATE

After God had eventually made man in another form, different from animals, He gave him the mandate, the exact reason He made him to be different, taking time to enumerate the components of the mandate. Furthermore, He gave an assurance of the capability of man to excel in the mandate by backing it up with His blessing.

Genesis 1:27-28 says,

> *"So God created man in His own image; in the image of God He created him; male and female He created them. Then God blessed them, and God said to them, "Be fruitful and multiply; fill the earth and subdue it; have dominion…"*

What else do we need to excel and prevail over the earth than this? We have the nature. We have the mandate. We have the blessing. And this means that we are fully equipped and empowered to exceed expectations in all the various aspects of the mandate that we have been given.

I am aware that there are some people who believe that the fall of man in the Garden has eroded both the nature of God in man and the power to execute the mandate given to him. And as such, they think that humans have become weaklings and minions of the earth rather than the ones having the dominion over it. But they err on three grounds.

First, even after the fall of man and especially after the flood that consumed the sinful inhabitants of the earth, God still restated His commitment to His original purpose for mankind on the earth.

Genesis 9:1-4,7 states:

> *"And God blessed Noah and his sons, and said unto them, Be fruitful, and multiply, and replenish the earth. And the fear of you and the dread of you shall be upon every beast of the earth, and upon every fowl of the air, upon all that moveth upon the earth, and upon all the fishes of the sea; into your hand are they delivered. Every moving thing that liveth shall be meat for you; even as the green herb have I given you all things... And as for you, be fruitful and multiply; Bring forth abundantly in the earth and multiply in it."*

What this reveals is that the place, purpose and function of man in relation to the earth did not die with the fall in the Garden. In fact, it was for the purpose of continuing the mandate that God instructed Noah to enter the ark with a pair each of other living creatures. He wanted the earth to remain, and as long as the earth remains, with man in it, then man who is part earth and part divine, will continue to be the appointed overseer.

Secondly, even if we should agree that the fall had brought devaluation to the nature and abilities of man, there still remains no reason to fail in our exercise of dominion over the earth since Christ has come to redeem us from the curses and limitations of the fall. Indeed this is where Christians have no excuse or explanation for not living a life of victory and dominion on earth. John 1:12 says that as many as believed in Jesus Christ, to them He gave power to become the sons of God – which makes us direct replicas of God on earth, just as Adam was.

Jesus Christ actually noted that a life of dominion is the central hallmark of anyone who receives Him. He says

"And these signs will follow those who believe: In My name they will cast out demons; they will speak with new tongues; they will take up serpents; and if they drink anything deadly, it will by no means hurt them; they will lay hands on the sick, and they will recover." (Mark 16:17-18).

He also says, "Behold, I give you the authority to trample on serpents and scorpions, and over all the power of the enemy, and nothing shall by any means hurt you." (Luke 10:19).

If this is not all-encompassing dominion, I don't know what it is.

Thirdly, right from the time of Adam till now, mankind has continued to exploit the earth with spectacular results and discoveries. Both Cain and Abel were successful workers of the earth, with one tilling the ground and the other domesticating and rearing animals. The case of Nimrod in Genesis is particularly worthy of mention. Even though his energies were mostly directed towards negative ventures, the Scripture still notes that he began to be a mighty man on earth (Genesis 10:8). This means that he exercised his physical and mental faculties to demonstrate control and dominion over the earth.

Let me especially point your attention to the building of the tower of Babel, which Nimrod masterminded. Even though it was a project that contradicted God's initial plan for mankind, God still attested to the infinite possibilities of the imagination of mankind to tailor the earth for their purpose. Note what God said in Genesis 11:6:

"Indeed the people are one and they all have one language, and this is what they begin to do; now NOTHING THAT THEY PROPOSE TO DO will be withheld from them..."

Fast-forward to the 21st century in which we are and see how far mankind has come in exploiting and configuring the earth. Countless inventions and discoveries have been made and are still being made. Interestingly, many of these are made by people who have no regard for God or think He even exists at all. Yet, they keep making all kinds of strides and advancements. Doesn't this confirm to you that man, even in his natural state, still retains much of his authority over the earth? How much more then should it be for us whose nature have been regenerated and who

55

have received the glorious, creative, transformative and unstoppable Spirit of the living God within us. What excuse do we have? Really we have none!

I will be mentioning the details of the mandate that God has given us as contained in Genesis 1:27-28, but let me quickly state that it's really saddening that many people – and more worrisome, even Christians – do not live to justify the purpose of the divine differentiation that God has made in creating us more unique than other lower creatures. We seem to be entirely contented with just doing the basic things of life – eating, drinking, breeding, having pleasures and dying. I'm not sure these activities require being made in the divine image because creatures that were total products of the earth do these things easily. And since to whom much is given, much is expected, it stands to reason that God had a higher purpose in making us and imbuing us with some of His own attributes. It should reveal to us that God indeed intends us to be gods of the earth. To do what He would have done from heaven.

According to a Christian writer, "The image of God in man…means that God made human beings, both male and female, to be created and finite representations (images of God) of God's own nature, that in relationship with Him and each other, they might be His representatives (imaging God) in carrying out the responsibilities He has given to them. In this sense, we are images of God in order to image God and His purposes in the ordering of our lives and carrying out of our God-given responsibilities."

COMPONENTS OF THE MANDATE

Let's have a closer look at the details of God's mandate to man as contained in Genesis 1:28.

"BE FRUITFUL"

God expects you as a human, and especially as a believer, to be fruitful on the earth. In other words, He expects you to bring forth - to be productive, to be successful, to excel on the earth. He wants you to be a generator, not just of new creatures (children) but of ideas and of inventions. He wants you to contribute your quota to the advancement of the earth.

To be fruitful can be put simply: "You have been made, make something too!" And the fruitfulness is general. Be fruitful mentally, physically, financially. In other words, barrenness, dryness or infertility is not your portion in any area of life. The Bible says,

> *"Blessed is the man Who walks not in the counsel of the ungodly, Nor stands in the path of sinners, Nor sits in the seat of the scornful; But his delight is in the law of the Lord, And in His law he meditates day and night. He shall be like a tree Planted by the rivers of water, That brings forth its fruit in its season, Whose leaf also shall not wither; And whatever he does shall prosper." (Psalm 1:1-3).*

Note also that since your fruitfulness is a divinely-ordained one, it does not know age limit. Psalm 92:13-14 says,

> *"The righteous shall flourish like a palm tree, He shall grow like a cedar in Lebanon. Those who are planted in the house of the Lord Shall flourish in the courts of*

our God. They shall still bear fruit in old age; They shall be fresh and flourishing."

So, despite being old in years, you can still be active for God and humanity. While your outward man may seem to be waning by reason of its natural limitation, your inward strength continues to be renewed from day to day.

The life of Caleb proved this to be true. Forty-five years after he had been among the spies sent to survey the Promised Land, he told Joshua,

> *"As yet I am as strong this day as on the day that Moses sent me; just as my strength was then, so now is my strength for war, both for going out and for coming in"* *(Joshua 14:11)*

In fact, it was at this 85 years of age that he was saying to Joshua, "give me this mountain." The life of Moses also exemplified this truth. As at the time of his death, it was said of him in Deuteronomy 34:7,

> *"Moses was one hundred and twenty years old when he died. His eyes were not dim nor his natural vigor diminished."*

Indeed, the Scripture has assured us that as our days are, so shall our strength be (Deuteronomy 33:25) – which means that the older you get physically, the better you become in usefulness. Again, our fruitfulness is not limited by location. As long as we are where God wants us to be, we shall excel. When Lot made the choice of pitching his tent towards the fertile lands of Sodom, he thought he had made the better deal and leaving Abraham with the rough end of the stick; yet it was as soon as Lot left him that

God appeared to him to assure him of boundless blessings and fruitfulness (Genesis 13:10-16).

"MULTIPLY"

This is a progression of fruitfulness. And for God to add multiplication to fruitfulness means that He wants us to not just be fruitful but to be exponentially so. He is not just interested in us having drops of mercy but showers of blessings in all that we do. This means that He is not the God of averageness but of superabundance. In every area of our lives, believers should not be managing to get by; we have the mandate and the blessing to prosper in our homes, workplaces and churches.

We have a classic example of this exponential increase in Genesis 26:12-13,

> *"Then Isaac sowed in that land, and received in the same year an hundredfold: and the Lord blessed him. And the man waxed great, and went forward, and grew until he became very great."*

That's the exact picture of exponential increase. Not only did he wax great but very great. What this means for us is that there is no room for mediocrity in the Kingdom. We are either at the top or we are nowhere at all; we are either at the forefront or we are nowhere!

For our children in school, to multiply is to go beyond merely passing their exams (fruitfulness) to excelling far above their peers. For those of us in business, it is to keep expanding in terms of quality, product lines, branches, employee strength, and turnover. For those in employment, it means going beyond doing our jobs well to becoming solution-providers and widely sought consultants, as well as getting multiple promotions. Above all, in our spiritual lives, it means all-round flourishing - in the fruit of the Spirit, gifts of the Spirit, soul-winning, demonstration of signs and wonders, multiple breakthroughs in mission and church planting and many more.

"FILL THE EARTH"

This again is a progression from multiplication. We are not just to increase and multiply, the impact and influence must resound throughout the earth. I pray that whatever success you're recording in your personal life, business, profession or church today, you are not just going to be a local champion but a global one.

It is the utmost desire of God that we continue to progress and expand without limit. Since there is no limitation with our God, there must be no limit to our success, progress, accomplishments and influence. The Bible says that men do not light a candle and put it under a basket; rather, they position it where it can be of maximum benefit to everyone (Matthew 5:15). That's where God wants each of us to be. That's where he wants our businesses, companies, services and churches to be. Where the glory of God upon our lives can reflect and radiate throughout the world. As God Himself has said,

> *"This people have I formed for myself; they shall shew forth my praise." (Isaiah 43:21).*

"SUBDUE"

To subdue is to conquer or bring into submission. That this significant point is being included in the mandate given to man portrays our God as not just being Almighty and all-knowing but also very practical. He made it clear from the outset that the tasks of being fruitful, multiplying, filling and dominating the earth will certainly involve some subduing – which means that it will not always be easy. It means that the earth will not always want to yield its secrets, treasures, riches and pleasantness. It will sometimes require us to harness all the physical, mental and emotional resources that God has deposited in us to be able to make it yield its benefits to us.

Sometimes, personal skills and know-how will not be enough; we need the support and collaboration of others. This is called "teamwork" or "networking". Sometimes, still, neither personal nor collaborative human effort will prove to be enough; we must return to God Himself to show us the secrets of the earth and the strategies we need to maximize its possibilities. It was this combination of human and divine effort that helped George Washington Carver (whose story we shall consider in detail later on) to discover the hidden possibilities of the peanuts, leading him to invent over a hundred products from the once despised crop.

The point here is, you cannot always expect the earth to be a blissful place for you without some physical, mental and spiritual effort on your part. This is how God Himself planned it for us. It is for this reason that He did not put precious stones and mineral resources on the surface of the earth. He hid them deep under – so that only those willing to pay the price of subduing will reap the benefits.

I think this is one of the areas where believers sometimes miss it and remain in a state of defeat or underachievement. The fact that we have been born again doesn't mean that everything will become automatically easy for us, or that God will automatically take care of all of our troubles. Not at all. God expects us to deploy all that He has deposited in us to deal with the challenges that can be humanly dealt with. He won't do for us what He has equipped us to do ourselves. What's the use of arming and kitting up a soldier without releasing him to have the battlefield experience?

God wasted no time in making man understand that subduing was a crucial component of his mandate. Soon after his creation, God had to bring the animals to him to name one after the other. God could have named them, but He left the task to Adam to let him know that he was fully in charge. We also learn a vital lesson from the life of Isaac, who despite being a child of promise, had to do a lot of work to make the earth habitable and enjoyable for himself. Particularly, in the case of the well which he was trying to dig, the Scripture says,

> *"Also Isaac's servants dug in the valley, and found a well of running water there. But the herdsmen of Gerar quarreled with Isaac's herdsmen, saying, "The water is ours." So he called the name of the well Esek, because they quarreled with him. Then they dug another well, and they quarreled over that one also. So he called its name Sitnah. And he moved from there and dug another well, and they did not quarrel over it. So he called its name Rehoboth, because he said, "For now the Lord has made room for us, and we shall be fruitful in the land."* (Genesis 26:20-22).

Did you see all that Isaac – a blessed child, with a great heritage – had to go through before getting to his Rehoboth? And did you see him crying helplessly to God to come and help him out? No – even though he knew he had the backing of the Almighty God, he had to be extra diligent and persistent to find his own comfortable place on the earth. There is a lot that the Lord wants us to emulate from these saints of old.

"HAVE DOMINION"

This is the crown and summation of the divine mandate and blessing of God upon humanity. Have dominion. Take charge. Rule your world! Note very importantly that the dominion that man is charged and blessed to have is an all-encompassing one. It is dominion over all the earth, which includes all things that pertain to the earth, whether its resources or the events that occur on it. Especially as children of God, we have the power and the mandate to determine the nature of events, policies, legislations to our own advantage and to the glory of God.

Jesus emphasized and amplified this dominion mandate of believers at different times. He says in Matthew 16:18,

"And I will give you the keys of the kingdom of heaven, and whatever you bind on earth will be bound in heaven, and whatever you loose on earth will be loosed in heaven."

In Mark 16:17-18, He says,

"And these signs will follow those who believe: In My name they will cast out demons; they will speak with

new tongues; they will take up serpents; and if they drink anything deadly, it will by no means hurt them; they will lay hands on the sick, and they will recover."

And yet again in Luke 10:19, He declares,

"Behold, I give you the authority to trample on serpents and scorpions, and over all the power of the enemy, and nothing shall by any means hurt you."

I have pointed out these verses from three different gospels to show you that even more than it was for Adam, God indeed wants us believers in Christ to wield such authority and dominion over the earth, that unbelievers like the Barbarians on the Island of Malta (Acts 28:1-5) will testify that we are extraordinary beings. Christ says whatsoever we bind or loose on earth shall be stamped in heaven. This means that we are the one who should be directing and dominating the affairs of the world from the spirit realm – deciding what should be or should not be. But the question is, how much of this authority are we wielding?

Sadly, again, as with other components of the divine mandate, the saints of old and sometimes the heathen seem to have better understanding of this authority and privilege more than modern day believers. We have the case of Joshua in the Bible, who like Moses who spoke to the earth, decided that nightfall should not come upon the earth until the Israelites had won against their enemies and it happened as he had decreed. In the case of Elijah too, he declared that there should be famine in the backslidden land of Israel for three and half years and it was so. Essentially, he declared that the earth should be starved of rain so that it would not produce any food and it happened as he declared. The Scripture even uses him to challenge us, saying:

> *"Elijah was a man with a nature like ours, and he prayed earnestly that it would not rain; and it did not rain on the land for three years and six months. And he prayed again, and the heaven gave rain, and the earth produced its fruit." (James 5:17-18).*

Now that's what I called dominion! Again, as I said before, since most us don't use the authority we have been given, Satan who likes to clone anything that God has done often empowers his agents to use the cloned version of our authority against us. I have heard of cases, especially in places like Africa, where people who are called "rain-makers" decide when rain should fall or not. And especially when churches want to hold outdoor programs, that's when mysterious rains fall to disrupt the events – simply because the people of God are dozing! May God rouse us from our slumber and make us take our rightful position of dominion in Jesus' name.

CHAPTER FOUR

BARRIERS TO DOMINION

One would think that with all that has been said about the wonders of the earth and the authority and power that have been conferred on believers to dominate and flourish in it, we should really be in control and be getting the best that God has implanted in our world. But the reality that stares us right in the face everywhere we turn proves otherwise.

Let's be sincere with ourselves. How much control do we, as believers, have over the resources underneath the earth or over the events that occur from day to day on it? How many riches in secret places have come into our possessions? How much of the glory of God reflects through our lives to the world around us? How much influence do we wield in our communities, schools and workplaces? How much have we been able to make the heathen tremble, as Moses did to the Egyptian magicians, so much that they will exclaim that the finger of God indeed works matchless wonders through our lives?

All around us are believers living under the yokes of failure, defeat, poverty, afflictions, oppressions, victimization, mediocrity, unfruitfulness, sicknesses, diseases, addictions and misfortunes. Rather than dominating the earth, the earth has subdued many, making them live a life of perpetual want amidst so much abundance. The birds of the air and the lilies of the field that are of far lesser value to God seem better fed, clothed and generally happier and less distressed than we who should be the lords of all. What could be wrong? As a prophet of old once asked,

"Is there no balm in Gilead, Is there no physician there? Why then is there no recovery for the health of the daughter of my people?" (Jeremiah 8:22).

Rightly should the prophet be worried, just as every vibrant believer should in these modern times. In Bible days, Gilead used to be well known for its spices and ointments, one of which was the "balm of Gilead" which was a popular ointment with excellent medicinal properties. Since it was a readily available provision for healing all sorts of infirmities, the prophet was worried that there should be so much sickness amidst so much medicine.

And so should we. When the children of a butcher feed on bones or when those of a fashion designer roam about in rags, it calls for serious concern. So, we return to our original question: Why are believers not having dominion over the earth?

IGNORANCE

The saying of the Scripture is true,

> *"...the heir, as long as he is a child, differeth nothing from a servant, though he be lord of all...Even so we, when we were children, were in bondage under the elements of the world" (Galatians 4:1-3).*

As long as believers remain ignorant of their Kingdom rights, privileges, authorities and responsibilities on earth, then we are bound to remain servants, even though God has made us lords.

Many believers think and live like the proverbial eaglet that was raised among chickens and thus kept feeding on dirt and worms until the day it was roused by another eagle in the sky. We seem not to realize that, aside from being humans with far higher capacity and authority to function above the lower creatures of the earth, we have also received the DNA of the Almighty God the moment we became born again. And with this automatically comes the mandate to live a life of distinction, excellence and all-round dominion.

> *"But you are a chosen generation, a royal priesthood, a holy nation, His own special people, that you may proclaim the praises of Him who called you out of darkness into His marvelous light; who once were not a people but are now the people of God, who had not obtained mercy but now have obtained mercy." (1 Peter 2:9).*

Becoming children of God makes us heirs of God. And an heir has access to all that belongs to the father. Besides, the Father has made several promises to us concerning the earth, which are ours to claim for enjoyment and dominion. But what happens when we do not know most of these promises, much less apply them? This is why God expresses concern about the inferior position that many of His children have allowed themselves to be relegated to due to self-inflicted ignorance. He says in Hosea 4:6,

"My people are destroyed for lack of knowledge..."

Besides, since to whom much is given, much is expected, our exalted position in Christ means that we have to operate on another level entirely, in our reasoning, aspirations, interactions and expectations. We are called to be transformed, rather than being conformed to the system around us. We are called to take charge, with the mandate of heaven, to enforce God's will on earth, not turn ourselves to ordinary earthlings who must be subject, like others, to the uncertainties of the earth. And with the fact that we have been given the keys to bind and lose whatsoever we will on earth, so much is expected of us. Sadly however many believers aren't aware of these rights and privileges. Some think power to exercise authority and dominion is only for pastors, church leaders and prayer-warriors. Thus the enemy keeps taking advantage of our ignorance and making us live the lives of helpless paupers in the midst of our rich inheritance.

Only our acquaintance with the truth of what God has said concerning us can make us function the way we should. Christ says,

"And you shall know the truth, and the truth shall make you free" (John 8:32).

COMPLACENCY

For many believers, the problem is simply complacency – the feeling of satisfaction with present attainment. It's natural that when we have no vision of where we should be, we will be comfortable with where we are. Many of us are not dominating because we have become too settled and relaxed in our comfort zones. We no longer task or stretch ourselves physically, mentally, professionally or spiritually. We do not want to exceed our present level of success and dominion in our various aspects of life. Thus our influence becomes grossly retarded and inhibited.

Here's what someone wrote about complacency, "Complacency is a blight that saps energy, dulls attitudes, and causes a drain on the brain. The first symptom is satisfaction with things as they are. The second is rejection of things as they might be. "Good enough" becomes today's watchword and tomorrow's standard. Complacency makes people fear the unknown, mistrust the untried, and abhor the new. Like water, complacent people follow the easiest course -- downhill. They draw false strength from looking back."

Isn't this the situation with many of us in our individual lives, families, churches and communities today? The sadder reality is that complacency not only leads to stagnancy but also retrogression and eventually death. This is why Jesus said,

> *"...whoever does not have, even what he has will be taken away from him" (Mark 4:25).*

We are losing our dominion because we are not using it as we should.

71

Retardation is an abnormality in the natural order for any living thing. It's either you grow or you die. It's either a river flows or it stinks. The reason Christianity has become a minor (and an endangered) religion in many parts of the so-called Arabic world where it was once the dominant religion was because Christians became complacent after the great missionary efforts of Paul and other earlier apostles.

Let's even leave the Arabic world and come to our so-called western world. Why are many churches being converted to cinemas, pub houses and even worse? It's because Christians have become too comfortable staying in our local corners. Yet, this was exactly why God scattered the builders of the tower of Babel by confusing their language. He didn't want them to settle in a place; He wanted them to fill the earth. This was why He also scattered the believers in the early church with persecution because the initial mandate they got was not to settle in Jerusalem and be arguing about who got food and who did not. The mandate for them (and for us) is to go into all the world, starting from Jerusalem (our local base).

UNBELIEF

Yes, let's face it, for some believers, many of what they read in Scriptures about saints of old exercising dominion over the earth – speaking to the ground, commanding the forces of nature and so on - are like myths and fairytales. Consequently, such disbelieving attitude makes us powerless and helpless. Unbelief paralyzes our dominion because it strips us of our connection with God, who is the source of our authority. Hebrews 11:6 says,

"But without faith it is impossible to please him: for he that cometh to God must believe that he is, and that he is a rewarder of them that diligently seek him."

Faith in God's word is the number one requirement for exploits on earth. It is by faith that we can understand that the earth is much more than a geological, non-living composition. It is by that same faith that we are to conquer and bring the earth to yield to our control. What you cannot believe you cannot achieve. Dominion is achieved in the spiritual realm before it manifests in the physical. Therefore, the moment we begin to take the truths that God has inspired for our learning to be mere fables or outdated experiences which are not "realistic" or compatible with our modern realities, then we lose our right to dominion.

Jesus told the disciples that once there is faith, they could say to any mountain to move (which I see as a way of reconfiguring or customizing the earth) and be cast into the sea and it would obey. But the condition is faith – which means that without faith it cannot be done. The reason Peter had dominion over nature as to walk on the sea was because he believed the words of Christ that he should come. But the moment he took his mind off the words and began to look at his surrounding and rationalizing the decision he was taking, he began to drown. What is drowning many of us today under the challenges of life is simply unbelief!

73

DESTRUCTIVE CONFESSIONS

Closely related to unbelief as a killer of our dominion over the earth is negative or destructive confession. It has been emphasized earlier that being created in the image and likeness of God, we are like gods on earth. Now, since everything that God created was called forth with the word of His mouth, it follows that we too can speak things into existence. That aside, we have also noted that the earth can hear, which means that with our mouth we can rouse it to work for us and with the same mouth we can rouse it to work against us. This is why the Bible declares,

"Death and life are in the power of the tongue,
And those who love it will eat its fruit" (Proverbs 18:21).

Those who love to use their tongues will definitely eat the fruit it rouses the earth to produce for them – whether it is the fruit of death or that of life. And for believers who have special authority, our declarations have exceptional powers. Yet, for most believers, it is the negative potential of the tongue upon the earth that they incite on themselves, speaking avoidable troubles and sorrows into their lives, especially when faced with challenges.

The misfortune that befell the Israelites, in which a journey which was predetermined to bring them into untold abundance and dominion ended in hardship and tragedy, was as a result of their destructive confessions. The same wilderness that was meant to be the bridge between their land of captivity and their land of dominion became the one that devoured them. It was the fruit of their confession. God told Moses,

"Say to them, 'As I live,' says the Lord, 'just as you have spoken in My hearing, so I will do to you: The carcasses of you who have complained against Me shall fall in this wilderness..." (Numbers 14:28-29).

It is the same with many believers. What we are today is an accumulation of what we declared upon ourselves yesterday and what we declare today will determine the shape of our future and what the earth brings forth for us. Therefore,

"He who would love life and see good days, let him refrain his tongue from evil..." (1 Peter 3:9).

OUTRIGHT SIN AND WORLDLINESS

This is another reality that cannot be denied. Our dominion over the earth is conditional. Sin can cause the earth to work against us, rather than working for us. It can cause the earth to devour us, rather than yielding its fruit to us. Isaiah 1:19 says,

"If ye be willing and obedient, ye shall eat the good of the land: But if ye refuse and rebel, ye shall be devoured with the sword: for the mouth of the Lord hath spoken it."

A reason many of today's Christians can't function with divine authority and dominion over the earth is because, unlike the saints of old, sinning and worldliness have come to be seen as a norm that cannot be done without. These are the days when sin is condoned and rationalized in our lives and churches with the excuse of "No one is perfect" and "Don't judge". And still, we wonder why we can no longer exert control and influence on the world.

Here is the answer: Nothing impairs spiritual dominion more than sinning. God is the source and backbone of our dominion and since sin constitutes rebellion against God, we become disconnected from Him and lose our dominion the moment we allow sin to have dominion over us. In fact, the reason the devil introduced sin into the world in the first place was to destroy man's dominion.

"The thief does not come except to steal, and to kill, and to destroy..." (John 10:10).

In the book, Pastor to Pastor, Erwin Lutzer revealed a startling discovery made by the late George Gallup (founder of the Gallup poll) concerning Christians. Lutzer writes: "Addressing a national seminar of Southern Baptist leaders, George Gallup said, "We find there is very little difference in ethical behavior between churchgoers and those who are not active religiously...The levels of lying, cheating, and stealing are remarkable similar in both groups." And this is why, like Samson in his fallen state, we have become like any other man.

What brings and sustains the glory of God upon our lives is righteousness. It is this glory that distinguishes and makes us to see the invisible and achieve the impossible. SIN is Satan's Identification Number – as 1 John 3:8 tells us. It invites Satan into our lives and makes us yield our birthright to him. We become unable to function optimally as we become severely downgraded and our strength becomes devoured.

Jesus says it clearly in Matthew 5:13,

"You are the salt of the earth; but if the salt loses its flavor, how shall it be seasoned? It is then good for nothing but to be thrown out and trampled underfoot by men."

Sin weakens, blindfolds, misleads, misinforms, relegates and destroys. It is debilitating and devastating. It turns giants to servants and reduces warriors to prisoners.

A graphic example of the incapacitating power of sin can be found in Joshua 7. The Israelites, in fulfillment of God's promise, had just conquered Jericho, beginning with its heavily fortified walls. However, contrary to God's instruction,

"Israel committed a trespass regarding the accursed things, for Achan the son of Carmi, the son of Zabdi, the son of Zerah, of the tribe of Judah, took of the accursed things; so the anger of the Lord burned against the children of Israel" (Joshua 7:1).

That automatically removed the glory of God from them and exposed them to a disgraceful defeat from Ai, a much smaller and less fortified city. It is in this same way that many believers remain failures and underachievers on earth, languishing under the yokes of afflictions and oppressions, rather than conquering and dominating - because they are toying with the "accursed" practices of sinning and worldliness.

SLOTHFULNESS

The love of slothfulness – which manifests in excessive love of sleep, fun, luxury, ease and comfort – is the reason many believers have become weaklings and minions, rather than having dominion over the earth. Especially in these days of abundant distractions from the entertainment industry and the social media, many believers have lost focus and forgotten their purpose. They get so entangled in feeding their eyes and pampering their flesh that they no longer have interest or willpower to subdue the earth and possess their rightful possessions.

This is why the Bible warns,

> *"Do not love sleep, lest you come to poverty; Open your eyes, and you will be satisfied with bread"* (Proverbs 20:13).

This is the only way to overcome spiritual and financial poverty. Yes, for even the birds of the air whom God provides food for, He doesn't drop it in their nest – they have to go look for it from the earth.

God has done it in such a way that nothing works on earth without work. He says,

> *"If anyone will not work, neither shall he eat."* (2 Thessalonians 3:10).

Even God had to work to create the earth and all the riches in it. And He has so done it in such a way that most of the riches of the earth are underneath it and those not underneath must be processed through work. He has done so to ensure that the earth must be tilled, subdued, cleared, watered and manured for it to yield bountiful harvests.

The message is clear – we must work hard to thrive on earth. And we must keep working to safeguard our place of dominion. However, for many believers physical and spiritual slothfulness continues to rob them of their place of dominion. They remain in a state of underachievement, stagnancy and retrogression, not because they are jinxed or unfortunate but because they cannot exert themselves to work their ways to their breakthroughs. They find it hard to discipline themselves to pray or fast. And they find it harder to put themselves through mental or physical rigor that will yield the expected blessings from the earth to them. Instead, they prefer wishing and daydreaming for success to come their way. Thus, despite having lots of privileges, promises and provisions from God, they remain in a state of spiritual, marital, material, professional and financial penury. Their case is aptly described in Proverbs 24:30-34,

"I went by the field of the lazy man, And by the vineyard of the man devoid of understanding; And there it was, all overgrown with thorns; Its surface was covered with nettles; Its stone wall was broken down. When I saw it, I considered it well; looked on it and received instruction: A little sleep, a little slumber, A little folding of the hands to rest; So shall your poverty come like a prowler, And your need like an armed man."

Did you see why I said that this man's case perfectly describes the state of many Christians today? Look at the glaring similarities. This man, like the typical believer, has a fertile field (which can be compared to the earth and its possibilities or to the talents and gifts that God has bestowed on every individual). That field could have yielded bountiful harvests of edible food crops and valuable fruits that could have made him prosperous and influential in the community. But because he couldn't be bothered to exert his mental and physical energy to cultivate, maintain and safeguard it, the field became overgrown with thorns and nettles (frustrations, failures and irritations) and the stone walls (which were to keep the field secure) had been broken down by invaders.

Isn't this the case with many believers today? Why is the earth yielding thorns and nettles for us, instead of pleasant and valuable fruits? Why are our lives filled with frustrations, failures and other abnormalities that are not in the original plan of God for us? And why are strangers invading the territory that belongs to us – making all the advancement, progress, breakthroughs and having all the influence? Why are we lagging behind while they take leading positions in all strata of society? In short, why, despite the declaration of Christ, is the children's bread being given to dogs? It's because

"the children of this world are in their generation wiser than the children of light." (Luke 16:8).

It is because believers have become too lazy to pray, to plan, to strategize and to work towards the fulfillment of their dreams. I pray the Lord will wake us up!

ACTIVITIES OF THE POWERS OF DARKNESS

There are times when the enemy fights viciously and ceaselessly to see that certain individuals, especially believers, never attain their rightful place of dominion in life. The reason is because the destiny and success of such have the potential to cause massive chaos in the demonic kingdom. Consequently, these wicked forces do all that's necessary to keep such people under the perpetual bondage of servitude. They do this mainly through spiritual sabotage, which comes in form of limiting strongholds. Except these activities of the enemy are paralyzed with the armor of God, the individual may find himself laboring so hard on the earth and getting so little in return. Wasted efforts, disappointments, frustrations and setbacks may continue to be the lot of such individuals, despite every attempt to break through in life.

The enemy may do this by sowing tares, in form of a curse, into the bloodline of the individual so that every member of the family becomes a potential victim. The Bible says in Matthew 13:24-28,

> *"Another parable He put forth to them, saying: "The kingdom of heaven is like a man who sowed good seed in his field; but while men slept, his enemy came and sowed tares among the wheat and went his way. But when the grain had sprouted and produced a crop, then the tares also appeared. So the servants of the owner came and said to him, 'Sir, did you not sow good seed in your field? How then does it have tares?' He said to them, 'An enemy has done this."*

Note that the purpose of the tares sown by the enemy was not really to kill the tares but to ensure that the man's harvest of wheat from the earth would continue to be drastically limited, regardless of how much effort he put into tending it. As long as the tares existed with the wheat, then the farmer would never get a commensurate reward for his labor. Like what they say in my place, he would continue to work like an elephant but get the meal of an ant. This is why some believers continue to wonder why all their righteous living, hard work and prayers seem not to be getting them the breakthrough and dominion that they desperately desire. The seed of the enemy has to be uprooted from their lives for the glory of God to shine upon them. Fortunately, the Lord has assured us that

"Every plant which My heavenly Father has not planted will be uprooted" (Matthew 15:13).

The enemy also does this by deliberately causing severe damage or havoc to an individual's livelihood or source of income, such that every opportunity or avenue for favor and blessing is blocked. We find a physical demonstration of this in the opposition of the envious Philistines against Isaac, as the Bible records,

"And Isaac dug again the wells of water which they had dug in the days of Abraham his father, for the Philistines had stopped them up after the death of Abraham." (Genesis 26:18).

Isaac had to undo the damage that the enemy had done to his inheritance, so as to continue to enjoy his produce from the earth (water). It is my prayer that the Lord will empower you to reverse every activity of the enemy in your life in Jesus' name.

CHAPTER FIVE

SECRETS OF DOMINION OVER THE EARTH

It is true that the earth can produce abundance and can also devour. We have seen in the previous chapter some factors that often make the earth devour and subdue the people of God rather than yielding to their dominion. Here, we shall unravel powerful principles that are bound to make the earth serve us and yield its best to us.

PARTNERSHIP WITH GOD

Even though God has made man the overseer of the earth, He is still the one in total control of the entire universe. For the earth in particular, the Bible says,

"The earth is the Lord's, and all its fullness, the world and those who dwell therein" (Psalm 24:1).

God made the earth, designed its shape, implanted its treasures and called forth its inhabitants. It is natural therefore for God to know more about the earth than we can ever know. Therefore, if we must prosper and flourish on this earth, we must cultivate an intimate relationship with this God.

Job 22:21-24 assures us:

> *"Now acquaint yourself with Him, and be at peace; thereby good will come to you. Receive, please, instruction from His mouth, and lay up His words in your heart. If you return to the Almighty, you will be built up; You will remove iniquity far from your tents. Then you will lay your gold in the dust, and the gold of Ophir among the stones of the brooks."*

There are a number of reasons we must partner with God to master the earth. I will be highlighting some of them here, but before I do, let me tell you an interesting story to illustrate why you must make this choice to have the dominion you desire.

A young man once owned a Ford vehicle that broke down on the side of a road. This man knew a lot about cars and especially this car, so he went to work. He tried different methods but each time he went back to try and crank the engine, it still wouldn't start. He tried again and again and, still, nothing happened. The car just wouldn't start.

A few minutes later, a large limousine pulled up beside him. Out stepped an old man who just stood and watched him for a few minutes. Finally, the old man looked at him and told him to adjust a specific part on the engine. The young man was initially skeptical as it seemed unreasonable to him that the part mentioned by the old man could have caused the vehicle to break down.

But then, after considering that he had tried other options without succeeding, he thought he might as well give the old man's advice a shot. So he adjusted the part, got in the car and sure enough, the engine cranked to life. He was surprised and asked the old man, "How did you know what to do?" The old man replied, "My name is Henry Ford and I invented this car."

Now, you know why partnering with God is the easiest and safest route to working the earth to your advantage. He "invented" the earth and knows all you need to know about it. Specifically, you need to partner with God for the following reasons:

1. The secrets of the earth belong to God. Deuteronomy 29:29 tells us,

> *"The secret things belong to the Lord our God, but those things which are revealed belong to us and to our children forever..."*

God knows what is yet to be discovered from the earth and where these hidden resources have been placed. You may, like Hagar, be seeing only a wilderness of death in a place where a well of life exists. Until God opens your eyes, you may continue to see nothing but adversities in a place of boundless opportunities! (Genesis 21:14-19). Moreover, God knows what part of the earth will favor you the most, especially in relation to your calling and purpose in life.

2. God knows what is yet to be discovered from the products of the earth.

While there are countless resources that are yet to be discovered within the earth, there are also boundless products that can be extracted from the plants, animals and other creatures and raw materials on the earth. God knows just what these potentials are. This was the secret that was revealed to George Washington Carver who discovered hundreds of products from the peanut, the potato and other crops that many had paid little or no attention to.

Carver had made Christ the Savior and Lord of His life much earlier and had been walking with Him daily. And even though he was a brilliant scientist who had obtained a master's degree in Agriculture, he made the wise decision to always acknowledge God as the true source of knowledge about the earth. According to him, "I love to think of nature as an unlimited broadcasting station, through which God speaks to us every hour if we will only tune in."

Armed with this vital secret, Carver would always talk to God every day to reveal the secrets of plants and vegetables to him. At a time, he had suggested to farmers in Alabama and nearby cities to plant more of peanuts to help them replenish the nutrients in their soil that were being depleted by heavy dependence on cotton. However, after some time, there was too much peanut to harvest and the people knew nothing else to do with it, apart from occasional eating.

What to do with the crop became a major concern and Carver, as usual, took the case to God. According to him, that same day, God led him back to his laboratory, which he had named "God's Little Workshop", and began to reveal to him products upon products that could be extracted from the peanuts. Carver experimented on these ideas and later published his findings in a pamphlet that was distributed to farmers throughout the United States. The findings led to hundreds of products and companies began to spring up to process the peanut. Peanut butter, insecticides, glue, rubber, and plastics are just a few of the many valuable peanut products discovered by Dr. Carver. In fact, by 1938, the once neglected peanut had become a $200 million industry and a chief product of Alabama!

That's what partnership with God can do in your life. Many other discoveries are yet to be made about the earth – and God is counting on you to be the next solution-provider. Start an intimate relationship with Him now!

3. He safeguards our footsteps from the habitations of cruelty.

Many people, including believers, have, in their quest for greener pastures, walked straight into the habitations of cruelty. We discussed earlier about these habitations while looking at the wonders of the earth. However, in this context, what I mean by habitation of cruelty is any place that may appear pleasant and attractive at a distance but would eventually lead to untold calamities and suffering.

Let me explain this further to help you understand. Satan sets traps for people of God all the time. However, when we are in tune with the Spirit of God, He guides our footsteps so we don't fall into the enemy's snares. However, when we deviate from God's will and follow our own carnal whims and fantasies, it becomes so easy to fall into avoidable accidents or even premature death on the surface of the earth.

Here are two quick examples. Do you remember what happened to Lot when he was to separate from Abraham? He made a rash and carnal decision to choose a place that he thought was best for him.

> *"And Lot lifted his eyes and saw all the plain of Jordan, that it was well watered everywhere (before the Lord destroyed Sodom and Gomorrah) like the garden of the Lord, like the land of Egypt as you go toward Zoar. Then Lot chose for himself all the plain of Jordan, and Lot journeyed east. And they separated from each other. Abram dwelt in the land of Canaan, and Lot dwelt in the cities of the plain and pitched his tent even as far as Sodom. But the men of Sodom were exceedingly wicked and sinful against the Lord."* (Genesis 13:10-13).

Lot made a seemingly fantastic choice which eventually turned out to be a habitation of destruction for him. It was the abundance of wealth that he and Abraham had that caused a crisis between their herdsmen, but by the time Lot would be leaving Sodom and Gomorrah, he couldn't take a single thing out. He even lost his wife as he fled the once attractive city. The earth had devoured all he had.

It was a great loss that Lot experienced, but that cannot be compared to the one experienced by Elimelech and his family. During a period of famine, he had left the land of Israel with his wife and two grown-up sons for the land of Moab. Within a short time however, the land had devoured him and his sons. Naomi, his wife, eventually

Secrets of Dominion Over the Earth

returned to the land of Israel a childless and penniless widow. According to her testimony,

> *"I went out full, and the Lord has brought me home again empty"* (Ruth 1:21).

It was indeed a pathetic narrative. The land had devoured all she had. This is what being in tune with God and His will at all times would have prevented.

4. He keeps us from unnecessary failures and wasted efforts.

Not only will partnership with God keep us from avoidable calamities but it will also keep us from losses that result from wasted efforts and investments. Many Christians wonder why they got involved in certain deals that backfired. Many companies wonder why they dabbled into certain product lines or open new branches that flopped spectacularly. Many churches wonder why some of their missionary efforts proved abortive and frustrating. Well, the answer lies in the truth that while every part of the world has been given to us, our conquest is meant to be a gradual, systematic and strategic one. What I mean by this is that while God wants us to conquer the earth, the conquest is not meant to be a random or haphazard experience.

Here is what God told the Israelites,

> *"I will send my fear before thee, and will destroy all the people to whom thou shalt come, and I will make all thine enemies turn their backs unto thee. And I will send hornets before thee, which shall drive out the Hivite, the Canaanite, and the Hittite, from before thee. I will*

89

not drive them out from before thee in one year; lest the land become desolate, and the beast of the field multiply against thee. By little and little I will drive them out from before thee, until thou be increased, and inherit the land" (Exodus 23:27-30, KJV).

Our God is not a God of confusion but of order. He does His things according to plan and proper timing. I have shown you the way He went about the work of creation - ensuring that whatever would sustain a creature was created first before the creature itself would be made. Many people wonder why the creation had to take God, who is the Almighty, six days. Well, there lies the answer. He could have created everything simultaneously in one day, but He chose to do otherwise to teach us very important lessons about life.

How does this apply to our partnership with God and our conquest of the earth? God knows the best time for us to harvest all that has been planted in the earth for us, and except we are in tune with Him, we may miss the timing and end up wasting our efforts. You know what happens when something is harvested at an inappropriate time. It's usually unpalatable or even poisonous.

Again, let me show you two examples on this. When Jesus was addressing the disciples, He says,

"Do you not say, 'There are still four months and then comes the harvest'? Behold, I say to you, lift up your eyes and look at the fields, for they are already white for harvest!" (John 4:35).

In other words, while the disciples were thinking the redemption of their nation was still some time in the future, Christ told them that the appropriate time had come.

You will also find that when Apostle Paul and his companions tried to enter into some cities to preach, the Holy Ghost prevented them from doing so, despite the fact that they were zealous to spread the gospel all over the world in accordance with the Great Commission (See Acts 16:7, for instance). What was responsible for this? Timing. Not that God wasn't interested in the salvation of those ignored cities, but the time for them to be conquered for Christ had not yet come. If Paul and his friends hadn't been in tune with God, they would have zealously gone into those cities and ended up wasting their time and efforts.

5. He places the mark of favor upon us so that whatever we do prospers.

The Psalmist declares in Psalm 1:1-3:

> *"Blessed is the man who walks not in the counsel of the ungodly, Nor stands in the path of sinners, nor sits in the seat of the scornful; but his delight is in the law of the Lord, and in His law he meditates day and night. He shall be like a tree planted by the rivers of water, that brings forth its fruit in its season, whose leaf also shall not wither; and whatever he does shall prosper."*

This is one of the greatest hallmarks of being in union with God. Wherever He leads you, you will prosper there. Whatsoever vocation He guides you to choose, you will excel therein. It doesn't matter what people think or the plan of the enemy against you, you will excel, because the mark of favor of God is upon you.

Observe the lives of many of the biblical patriarchs, and you will find this principle at work. Joseph was highly favored by his father above his brethren, even though he was neither the first nor the last born. Even when his brothers enviously sold him and he became a servant in Potiphar's house, he still prospered and became a leader there. According to his testimony, all that belonged to his master was in his care. Again, when Potiphar's wife lied against him and had him thrown into prison, he ended up becoming the overseer of all the other prisoners. Not only that, the first day he ever stepped into Pharaoh's palace, he demonstrated such remarkable excellence that the special position of Prime Minister was carved out exclusively for him and he became the deputy ruler of the entire land of Egypt.

So we find that the same principle of favor worked upon Joseph's life everywhere he went. Whether he was at home or in a strange land; whether he was in a prison or in the palace, God's hand of favor was mighty upon him because he had a special regard for God.

It is the same thing we find in the life of Abraham. A glaring instance is the outcome of the tussle between his herdsmen and those of Lot. As we observed earlier, when Lot was given the opportunity to choose the portion of land that interested him, he took his time to examine the entire landscape and eventually settled for the part that he considered most fertile and alluring, leaving the terrain that he considered unpleasant and least promising for Abraham. Yet Abraham never complained, because his mind was rested on the Almighty who had been with him from the beginning. And, as usual, God did not disappoint him.

"And the Lord said to Abram, after Lot had separated from him: "Lift your eyes now and look from the place where you are—northward, southward, eastward, and westward; for all the land which you see I give to you and your descendants forever. And I will make your descendants as the dust of the earth; so that if a man could number the dust of the earth, then your descendants also could be numbered. Arise, walk in the land through its length and its width, for I give it to you." (Genesis 13:14-17).

Children of God don't reject or protest against transfers in their places of work or missionary assignments (except the Spirit of God strongly leads them to) because they know that the mark of greatness is upon them. They will succeed wherever they are placed. As the Lord assured Joshua,

"Every place that the sole of your foot will tread upon I have given you..." (Joshua 1:3).

PRAYER

A man who will have unusual dominion on earth must have unceasing communion with heaven. As I have mentioned before, the earth overflows with wonders and mysteries, which can be best revealed to us by God. He has specifically told us how we can get such revelations from Him:

"Call to Me, and I will answer you, and show you great and mighty things, which you do not know". (Jeremiah 33:3).

There are many great and mighty things about our earth that will remain undiscovered and untapped until we pray. There are situations and conditions that will remain unchanged and unfavorable until we pray.

Of course, I have hinted on the importance of prayer when I cited how people like George Washington Carver became great inventors and discoverers. But my emphasis here goes beyond asking God to show us things; it is about making prayer our natural habit. This is necessary because in the place of prayer, we get much more than what we ask for. We even receive revelations that we did not ask for but which the Holy Spirit considers necessary for our attention.

The reason people like John Knox could wield so great influence upon the world was because they could pray. It was John Knox, who, like Elijah of old, wanted to shape the course of events in his country so badly that he persistently besought God, saying "Give me Scotland, else I die!" So mighty was his influence upon his country that the reigning monarch, Mary, Queen of the Scots, declared, "I fear the prayer of Knox more than all the armies of England put together". This is what I call the believers' dominion on earth and it confirms the saying that he who can kneel before God can stand before any man.

We must learn to pray without season to obtain and maintain victory over the earth. Prayer can reshape our destinies and reconfigure the earth around us. Prayer makes mountains low; it lifts up valleys and straightens crooked places. Jabez' curse was removed, Abraham's reproach was taken away, Jacob's name was changed and Hannah received her long awaited miracle – all in the pace of prayer. And we can have the same victory today over the earth, if we can pray.

The reason many believers are victimized, oppressed and brutalized in many parts of the world is largely because of the prayerlessness of the church. We find a similar thing in the time of the Early Church. When James the Elder was arrested and imprisoned by Herod, we have no record that the Church prayed intensely on his behalf. So, it was easy for Herod to have him beheaded, to the delight of the enemies. However, by the time he imprisoned Peter, another pillar in the church, then the Church woke up from its slumber. Here is the account in Acts 12:1-5:

> *"Now about that time Herod the king stretched out his hand to harass some from the church. Then he killed James the brother of John with the sword. And because he saw that it pleased the Jews, he proceeded further to seize Peter also. Now it was during the Days of Unleavened Bread. So when he had arrested him, he put him in prison, and delivered him to four squads of soldiers to keep him, intending to bring him before the people after Passover. Peter was therefore kept in prison, but constant prayer was offered to God for him by the church."*

The result of the Church's unceasing prayer was that, unlike James who was killed so brutally, Peter was miraculously released from prison. Indeed, wonders happen when we pray!

I must also add, very importantly, that it is only by prayers that we can dislodge the activities of the wicked ones who do not want us to prosper on the earth. As I mentioned

95

earlier, there are forces who would rather have us live a miserable, defeated and frustrated life on earth; after all, the ultimate purpose of the enemy on earth is to steal, to kill and to destroy (John 10:10). And the surest way we can subdue him is to invoke the superior firepower of the Almighty God, using the weapon of prayer.

"For the weapons of our warfare are not carnal, but mighty through God to the pulling down of strong holds" (2 Corinthians 10:4).

PRAISE AND THANKSGIVING

There are times when prayer has to be complemented with praise and thanksgiving for it to have maximum impact over the earth. And there are times when all we need is just praise and thanksgiving alone to get the earth to tremble and come to our aid or bend to our will. Psalm 67:5-7 tells us how it works:

"Let the people praise thee, O God; let all the people praise thee. Then shall the earth yield her increase; and God, even our own God, shall bless us. God shall bless us; and all the ends of the earth shall fear him" (KJV).

When we cultivate the habit of praising God and appreciating Him for His goodness in our lives - not only when we are in church but every day of our lives – then we compel the earth to yield its abundance to us. Goodness and mercy will follow us all the days of our lives. Ways will appear for us in seemingly dry lands and rivers of water will burst forth from every situation that appears like a desert to us. The Lord has done it many times before and He will do it again and again. There have been numerous testimonies of breakthroughs through praises and thanksgiving. Many challenges that refused to yield to ordinary prayers have crumbled when the people of God began to praise God.

A graphic depiction of how our praises and thanksgiving can stir the earth to our favor is recorded in Acts 16:25-26,

> *"And at midnight Paul and Silas prayed, and sang praises unto God: and the prisoners heard them. And suddenly there was a great earthquake, so that the foundations of the prison were shaken: and immediately all the doors were opened, and every one's bands were loosed."*

As Paul and Silas prayed and sang praises to God in their midnight hour, the earth responded by destroying the very foundation of their captivity, crashing down their prison doors and breaking off their chains. This and many more can happen in our lives too if we will maintain an attitude of gratitude to God at all times, rather than complaining or making negative confessions.

COMMANDING THE EARTH

This is another powerful way of taking dominion over the earth. We must be able to issue out commands to it. It is not every time that we must pray prayers of petition; there are times when we must, like Joshua who spoke to the sun and the moon, and Jesus who spoke to the fig tree, prophesy and decree what we what from the earth. We have read earlier how Christ promised to give us the keys to bind or loose whatever we wish on earth. Prior to that, God had promised us in Job 22:28 (KJV),

"Thou shalt also decree a thing, and it shall be established unto thee: and the light shall shine upon thy ways."

So then, since we serve a God who cannot lie, then we must go ahead to decree and call forth whatsoever we want from the earth, just as God did at the time of creation. We must decide and decree the kind of life we want on earth, rather than letting the earth dictate to us. When we leave the earth to decide for us, what we are likely to get from it will be worthless things, just like the farmer that leaves his farm to fate will get nothing but weed. As it is said, "Life doesn't give you what you deserve but what you DEMAND!"

There is something we must learn from the experience of Ezekiel on this. In Ezekiel 37:1-4, we are told,

"The hand of the Lord came upon me and brought me out in the Spirit of the Lord, and set me down in the midst of the valley; and it was full of bones. Then He caused me to pass by them all around, and behold, there were very many in the open valley; and indeed they were very dry. And He said to me, "Son of man, can these bones live?" So I answered, "O Lord God, You know. Again He said to me, "Prophesy to these bones, and say to them, 'O dry bones, hear the word of the Lord!'"

There is an instructive message here which most of us don't pay attention to in looking at this Scripture passage. Here was Ezekiel, a prophet of God, before a multitude of dry bones and when it was time to decide whether the bones should live or remain dead, his answer was that only God could decide that. And that's what most of us do. Situations we have been empowered to command and decide, we wait for "God's will" to be done and things continue to deteriorate.

As I mentioned earlier, God won't do for us what He has equipped us to do for ourselves. In the particular instance that we are considering, God instantly told Ezekiel, "Prophesy to these bones…" This is exactly what many of the abnormalities around us require. They are waiting for us to decree what we want with them, while we keep waiting for God to do it for us. We must begin to use the authority that we have been given. Decree. Prophesy. Bind. Loose. And the earth will obey you!

TAKE STEPS OF FAITH AND INVEST

As we are guided by the Spirit of God, we must be willing to take decisive steps of faith to be able to have the dominion that is our heritage. Every part of the earth is ours to explore and we cannot afford to be fearful or complacent. We cannot take possession of the earth that we're not willing to explore. We cannot be in control when we are hidden in our cocoon. We must launch out, reach out and explore new horizons as we are guided by the Holy Spirit.

Our long-awaited breakthrough in ministry, career or business may be in the very next move we are going to make. How then are we to get it if we don't make a move? It was God Himself who told the Israelites,

"You have dwelt long enough at this mountain. Turn and take your journey, and go to the mountains of the Amorites, to all the neighboring places in the plain, in the mountains and in the lowland, in the South and

on the seacoast, to the land of the Canaanites and to Lebanon, as far as the great river, the River Euphrates. See, I have set the land before you; go in and possess the land which the Lord swore to your fathers..." (Deuteronomy 1:6-8, KJV).

Faith without action is dead. So, if we are confident that as children of God, the earth and its blessings are our heritage, then we must back up our faith with necessary actions. In the above passage, the Israelites knew that they had been promised all the lands round about them, but they were not willing to take the necessary steps to possess their possessions. This was why God had to order them to action. Once God has given us His assurance on any move, then we must not hesitate, regardless of what prevailing circumstances may be. We must walk by faith and not by sight.

In this regard, we must learn from Isaac. When he was about to make a move to the land of Egypt during a famine and God warned him not to, he promptly obeyed. But not only did he obey and believed God to bless him, he went ahead to take an action of faith and he got the blessings of God upon him in multiple dimensions. Genesis 26:12-13 says,

"Then Isaac sowed in that land, and received in the same year an hundredfold: and the Lord blessed him. And the man waxed great, and went forward, and grew until he became very great: For he had possession of flocks, and possession of herds, and great store of servants: and the Philistines envied him."

This is a breakthrough secret we have to learn as believers.

We cannot always wait for a "favorable" time before we take necessary actions. Isaac sowed into a seemingly barren land and became very prosperous because he was sure that God was with him. The people who control the biggest companies of the world today invested when things were not so smooth. People who owned the largest and most widespread churches in the world do so because they took the risk of church planting in barren lands. The colonialists who went to Africa and other parts of the world were able to exert their influence because they took the risk to explore. Missionaries who took over many parts of the world for Jesus did so because they took risk. Mary Slessor was able to do exploits in Nigeria and stopped the killing of twins in Calabar, at a time when the country had not become so developed. Till today, her influence continues to be felt.

We also need to take a cue from our Lord and Master, Jesus Christ. At a time in His ministry, He became so popular in a particular place that people told Him,

"Everyone is looking for You." (Mark 1:37).

It is in situations like this that the line is drawn between those who have real dominion and those who do not. Left to some people, the statement in the above verse would have been the exact confirmation they needed to conclude that they had arrived; that they had become truly successful. And so they get carried away by their present success and forget that each achievement or breakthrough is supposed to be a stepping stone to a greater one that God has in store. This is why many believers and churches remain confined. But, trust Jesus, His answer was powerfully instructive:

"And he said unto them, Let us go into the next towns, that I may preach there also: for therefore came I forth." (verse 38).

So, rather than settling in one place or position to enjoy His success, Jesus said the best thing to do was to go for more conquest over the earth. This should be our watchword always. If we must have constant dominion over the earth, then we must take constant actions to POSSESS it!

PART 2

TAKE CHARGE, RULE THE SEAS

CHAPTER SIX

MYSTERIES OF THE SEAS

I am sure that, like the two disciples that Jesus Christ met on the road to Emmaus (Luke 24:13-32), your heart must have been tremendously stirred by the great and mighty secrets that the Lord has revealed to us about the earth. The greater news however is that there is even more to come, as we explore the wonders of the sea and how to exercise our God-given dominion over it. By "the sea" here, I am referring to the bodies of water generally, including rivers, oceans, seas and the likes.

For starters, bodies of water aren't just composed of water. They represent and harbor so much more. As a science researcher has once explained, "Those large, beautiful bodies of water are home to an infinite number of strange creatures and bewildering phenomena. The average ocean depth is 14,000 feet deep — that leaves a lot of room for the mysterious, the mythical and everything in between."

Confirming this, Fred Gorell, the head of public affairs at the National Oceanic and Atmospheric Administration's Ocean Exploration and Research division, recently told a news medium, "The ocean is 95% unexplored, unknown, unseen by human eyes. Every time we go off on an expedition, we see something new..."

If anyone should be able to testify that the sea harbors much more than the creatures and plants that most of us have often associated with it, it should be Christopher Columbus, the famous Spanish explorer, whose historic voyages opened up regular contact between America and Europe – and thus changed the course of history. He had been an explorer for years and sailed the oceans quite often. He thought he knew all about the seas, until he had a very peculiar encounter which he later recorded in his diary. Washington Irving, in his 1841 book, *History of the Life and Voyages of Christopher Columbus*, reproduced Columbus observation thus:

"On the 13th of September, in the evening, being about two hundred leagues from the island of Ferro, Columbus for the first time noticed the variation of the needle; a phenomenon which had never before been remarked. He perceived about nightfall, that the needle, instead of pointing to the North Star varied about half a point, or between five and six degrees to the northwest, and still more on the following morning. Struck with this circumstance, he observed it attentively for three days, and found that the variation increased as he advanced. He at first made no mention of this phenomenon, knowing how ready his people were to take alarm, but it soon attracted the attention of the pilots, and filled them with consternation. It seemed as if the very laws of nature were changing as they advanced, and that they were entering another world, subject to unknown influences..."

The particular area of the ocean where Columbus and his companions had this bizarre encounter has come to be known as the Bermuda Triangle or the Devil's Triangle. It lies in the North Atlantic Ocean between Bermuda, Miami and San Juan, Puerto Rico. It has become a subject of considerable attention in modern times because a number of aircraft and ships are said to have disappeared within the area under mysterious circumstances. In fact, to date, the compass does not show towards North once it is within the strange region. For years, diverse clarifications and counter-arguments have been given about this mysterious part of the ocean, with none proffering a conclusive explanation.

But let's put Bermuda Triangle aside for now and consider something else. When Jules Verne wrote in his classic sci-fi novel, "20,000 Leagues under the Sea" about a certain "milk sea" - a portion of the sea which at night produces an intense glow likened to a cloudbank or snowfield for as far as the eye can see - many scientists simply ignored it as one of the typical maritime fables often told by sailors. These sailors of old sometimes told tales of suddenly encountering "pale, milky, glowing waters," but nobody took them seriously. However, in January 1995, things took a different turn. A report from the ship, SS Lima, while sailing through the Indian Ocean, showed the milky sea to be astoundingly real.

The verbatim report read: "22:00 local time on a clear, moonless night a whitish glow was observed on the horizon and, after 15 min of steaming, the ship was completely surrounded by a sea of milky-white color with a fairly uniform luminescence. The bioluminescence appeared to cover the entire sea area, from horizon to horizon . . . and it appeared as though the ship was sailing over a field of snow or gliding over the clouds."

Can you imagine that? A huge, cloud-like area on the high seas? This astonishing discovery, an enormous patch of glowing sea, covering an area as large as the entire state of Connecticut, has been confirmed by other explorers and scientists since then. And as usual, many attempts have been made to explain the mystery, without much success. In fact, I like the conclusion drawn by one of the lead scientists that have attempted to explain the phenomenon: "There are still far more questions than answers surrounding milky seas. We have gained a new sense for how very little indeed we really know about the place we call 'home."

True to the admission of the scientist, there is indeed very little we know about the sea or the bodies of water in general. For us believers, this ignorance has not only deprived us of many of the blessings that the Lord has embedded in these massive part of the universe but it has also led to a lot of havoc being unleashed upon the church by the forces that control these waters. Fortunately, God, the creator, has revealed to us all we need to know about the sea in the Scripture. This is why we must return to the Word to discover the hidden truths about it and how we can use these truths to not only gain mastery over the sea and its mysteries, but to also do exploits in our lives, homes, churches and communities.

WONDERS OF WATERS

1. Waters have massive deposits of riches.

We serve an awesome God who is full of wonders and boundless in riches. Just as He has loaded the earth with inexhaustible riches for the benefit of mankind, He has equally hidden an immeasurable amount of riches and resources underneath the seas and oceans of the world.

To begin with, sea creatures, such as the different species of fish provide massive income for individuals, organizations, communities and countries each year. In fact, a reliable report has it that about 200 billion pounds of fish are caught each year, yet the supply never ceases. Much more than that, the sea harbors an infinite amount of mineral resources - manganese, copper, nickel, iron and cobalt – as well as crude oil that have become the mainstays of many economies of the world.

Findings have equally shown that since industrial extraction of oil began in the mid-19th century, over 147 billion tons of oil have been pumped from bodies of water around the world. And yet, both crude oil and other resources are just raw resources. The products that are extracted from these resources that have been mentioned are what most companies and peoples of the world depend on for survival and for commerce. In fact, to be more precise, the waters of the earth are magnificent resources of wealth themselves, as a vast amount of wealth is not only obtained from them but also transported on them every day.

We find a seemingly symbolic message on how God has loaded the sea with riches with the account in Matthew

17:24-27. Tax collectors had come to demand for temple tax from Peter and Jesus. And whether there was money in the house or not, we cannot absolutely tell. But Jesus gave an instruction to Peter that should open our eyes to a life-changing truth about the waters around us. Here's what He told Peter,

> *"Go to the sea, cast in a hook, and take the fish that comes up first. And when you have opened its mouth, you will find a piece of money; take that and give it to them for Me and you"* (verse 27).

I know this is probably not your first time of reading this verse. But take another look at it. Why, without hesitation, would Jesus instruct Peter to go to the sea and get money from the mouth of a fish? Let not the message be lost on you. There is vast wealth to sustain the world and save anyone from the embarrassment of financial lack in the sea. And millions of people have found this to be true and are enjoying untold riches from the sea. And you know what? God has promised to turn these riches to you, as a believer. He says in Isaiah 60:5 (please, say a big amen to every part of this promise as you read):

> *"Then you shall see and become radiant, and your heart shall swell with joy; Because the abundance of the sea shall be turned to you, the wealth of the Gentiles shall come to you."*

God has made it clear – not only will He guide you on how to make riches from the sea, but He will also make wealth from unexpected places across the sea to come to you. I pray that you begin to receive calls of blessings from overseas from today in Jesus' name.

The message in all this for you, child of God, is that with all the resources that your Father has surrounded you with, you should not live in want. Why should the church of God continue to be seen as the gathering place of paupers and beggars when our Father has generously provided all that we need and has equally promised to turn this wealth to us? We must know what belongs to us and claim it by faith!

2. Waters have cities with gates and rulers.

Now, we are getting to deeper revelations about the sea and you must pay particular attention. First, let's look at something significant in Nahum 2:6-7:

"The gates of the rivers are opened, and the palace is dissolved. It is decreed: She shall be led away captive, she shall be brought up; and her maidservants shall lead her as with the voice of doves, beating their breasts".

The history of the entertainment world is replete with movies and cartoons featuring so-called "mermaids" with supernatural powers that are often presented in appealing forms. Many people consider these presentations to just be for fun, but note this: as the above Scripture reveals, there are actually rulers of the marine world, which are usually females. To be added to that is that, contrary to what the entertainment industry shows, the rulers of the marine kingdom are not in any way benevolent; they are about the most malevolent and destructive forces that Satan has in his kingdom. Of course, they may take on attractive forms when they manifest in the human world, but that's where the similarity ends.

The point here is that, as with other parts of the universe, bodies of water are not composed of just hydrogen and oxygen (H_2O) as scientists would like us to believe; they have a deeply spiritual existence and essence. A key part of this spiritual essence is that waters are independent habitations. Just as the world of the earth exists, so also is the world of the waters. In this world are demonic beings whose world closely resembles that which we have on earth. Structures, governments, commerce and daily activities are conducted by these beings. In fact, as we shall be seeing later on, many of the activities, customs, traditions, practices, influences, behaviors, fashions and entertainments on earth are mere replicas of what obtains in this oceanic world.

The only difference between the world on earth and the one in the waters is that while many people on earth do not understand the reason they do most of the things they do and sometimes choose to live purposelessly, the inhabitants of the water kingdom have a singular purpose, to which they are wholeheartedly dedicated – inventing and introducing destructive influences into the world on earth, to corrupt the souls of men, keep them in perpetual bondage and ensure they end their lives and spend eternity with the devil.

So, as Nahum shows us, waters of the earth have gates – that is, entry and exit points – like a typical city on earth. And there are palaces of the rulers there.Ezekiel 29:3 further confirms this truth when it declared:

> *"Speak, and say, 'Thus says the Lord God: "Behold, I am against you, O Pharaoh king of Egypt, O great monster who lies in the midst of his rivers, who has said, 'My River is my own I have made it for myself.'"*

Here, the Lord makes it clear to us that not only can a river have a ruler but also that marine spirits can be so proud, possessive and stubborn to deal with.

3. Waters can control the lives of individuals, communities and families.

Since there are beings in most bodies of water, whose primary purpose of existence is to influence and keep people in perpetual bondage, it often happens that some of their agents on earth (witchdoctors, spiritualist, false prophets) often help the marine powers to tighten their grip over individuals, families and communities on earth by instructing or encouraging them to initiate or perpetuate relationship with these water spirits through rituals. This helps to keep such people in perpetual bondage.

There are communities in many African countries where annual celebrations and sacrifices are made to celebrate or appease a certain body of water. There are those who do ritual bathing (different from that which God Himself or a prophet of God instructs). There are even cases in which babies born in certain communities are required to be bathed in certain bodies of water for the ostensible reason of establishing or maintaining affinity with the community. Yet, in the real sense, it is the demon in the river that is being further empowered. The implication is that the course of lives and destinies of such individuals become continually vulnerable to the activities and operation of such spirit.

I even heard of a community in which this practice is so strong that even if a child is born in a faraway land, he must be brought back to be bathed in the river. And there are also those who drink and bathe in certain rivers because such waters are said to possess special powers to give healing or fertility. Unknown to such people, they are simply dedicating themselves and their children to the captivity of the marine powers and the effect may linger on for many years.

Take the case of Moses for instance. When he was born, his parents had defied the orders of the then Pharaoh to have all Hebrew male babies killed. He had been nursed at home for some time before the parents decided one day that it had become too risky to keep him at home. Thus, they kept him in a well-protected basket and placed him at the bank of the Nile, around the area where Pharaoh's household frequented for bathing and other purposes. It happened that Pharaoh's daughter went to the river that day to have her bath and she saw the baby and ultimately adopted him. Now, this is significant. The Nile was a river thought to have special powers. In fact, Pharaoh himself bathed in the river daily to renew his strength. To Pharaoh's daughter, therefore, the baby she found was a gift from the river. She gave him the name, "Moses", which means "Drawn Out of Water" – or to put it more clearly, "A Gift from the River."

Essentially, Pharaoh's daughter dedicated Moses to the river spirit. This would eventually have a serious effect on Moses' life, causing him to sometimes manifest uncontrolled anger. Uncontrolled anger is one of the manifestations of the marine spirit and this character flaw almost derailed Moses' destiny. It was in his fiery anger that he killed an Egyptian who was fighting with a Hebrew man and had to flee the land of Egypt. This brought a serious delay in the fulfillment of his destiny as he had to be in hiding for

40 years before God appeared to him to not only commission him to be the deliverer of the Israelites but also empower him to destroy the dominion of the marine spirit over his life.

Many people born in riverine areas or have been dedicated to water spirits often have challenges serving God effectively because of the influence of the marine forces. In fact, they often do all they can to keep themselves away from God and they battle with not just anger but lust and sexual immorality.Revelation 17:1-2 says,

> *"Then one of the seven angels who had the seven bowls came and talked with me, saying to me, "Come, I will show you the judgment of the great harlot who sits on many waters, with whom the kings of the earth committed fornication, and the inhabitants of the earth were made drunk with the wine of her fornication."*

I will be dwelling more on the pervasive influence of this lustful spirit in these last days, especially in the church. But let me emphasize that deliverance from the power of the marine spirit can be intense, but as we have seen from the example of Moses, it is absolutely necessary to get this deliverance so as not to have one's destiny hijacked and wasted. In the case of Moses, when the Lord sent him back to Egypt, he had to perform some miracles, two of which were important for his own victory.

The first miracle that Moses performed that was symbolic to his victory was turning the rod of Aaron to a snake. Exodus 7:8-12 reads,

> *"Then the Lord spoke to Moses and Aaron, saying, "When Pharaoh speaks to you, saying, Show a miracle*

*for yourselves,' then you shall say to Aaron, Take your
rod and cast it before Pharaoh, and let it become a
serpent." So Moses and Aaron went in to Pharaoh, and
they did so, just as the Lord commanded. And Aaron
cast down his rod before Pharaoh and before his servants,
and it became a serpent.*

But Pharaoh also called the wise men and the sorcerers;
so the magicians of Egypt, they also did in like manner
with their enchantments. For every man threw down his
rod, and they became serpents. But Aaron's rod swallowed
up their rods."

This miracle represents victory over the serpent, which
echoes God's pronouncement in Genesis 3:15. Specifically,
for this context, the ruling spirit in Egypt was a serpent
which is another representation of the marine spirit. On
the crown of Pharaoh was a symbolic image of a serpent.
Moses turning the rod to a serpent and making it swallow
up the serpents produced by Pharaoh's magicians was a
way of showing dominion over the power of Pharaoh
obtained from the River Nile, as well as showing dominion
over the marine spirit controlling the nation.

The second significant miracle was the turning of the
waters of Egypt, especially, the River Nile, into blood.

*"And the Lord spake unto Moses, Say unto Aaron, Take
thy rod, and stretch out thine hand upon the waters of
Egypt, upon their streams, upon their rivers, and upon
their ponds, and upon all their pools of water, that they
may become blood; and that there may be blood
throughout all the land of Egypt, both in vessels of wood,
and in vessels of stone. And Moses and Aaron did so, as*

the Lord commanded; and he lifted up the rod, and smote the waters that were in the river, in the sight of Pharaoh, and in the sight of his servants; and all the waters that were in the river were turned to blood. And the fish that was in the river died; and the river stank, and the Egyptians could not drink of the water of the river; and there was blood throughout all the land of Egypt." (Exodus 7:19-21).

If you observe closely, you would see that even though all the waters in Egypt were turned into blood, there is constant reference to "the river". This is the River Nile, the most important river to Pharaoh and the Egyptians. Moses, in turning the river to blood, was a way of confronting the power that had been having a negative influence on his destiny and gaining dominion over it. It was thus a symbolic victory for Moses and the people he needed to deliver. What this should tell you is that, like Moses, you need to confront whatever influence that affects your life and destiny negatively, using the power and the authority that God has given you as a believer. You cannot afford to run or hide or pretend that the challenge is not there. What you don't confront, you can never conquer.

Before, I proceed to the next point, I need to show you another proof of how the waters can affect an entire community or nation.

"And the men of the city said unto Elisha, Behold, I pray thee, the situation of this city is pleasant, as my lord seeth: but the water is naught, and the ground barren. And he said, Bring me a new cruse, and put salt therein. And they brought it to him. And he went

*forth unto the spring of the waters, and cast the salt in
there, and said, Thus saith the Lord, I have healed these
waters; there shall not be from thence any more death
or barren land. So the waters were healed unto this day,
according to the saying of Elisha which he spake"* (2
Kings 2:19-22).

Now, looking at this passage, you may ordinarily not think
much of the events here, until you take a closer look at it.
Here was a city that was made to be pleasant and every
other thing about it attested to this. But there was a major
problem with the waters and this problem caused the land
to be barren and many people to die – until Elisha rose
to the occasion by the power of God Almighty.

What this implies is that the forces of the marine world
can have a major impact over a whole community or
nation. An entire city or community can be bound by the
power of lust and sexual immorality (Jude 1:7). Decisions
taken under the waters can plunge an otherwise blessed
city or glorious church into a place of immoralities,
calamities, unfruitfulness and all-round misery. It is for
this reason that we as believers must take our stand and
resist and reverse every negative influence from the waters
with the authority of the Most High God.

4. The sea can speak and it can hear.

Just as we have established about the earth, the waters also
have a personality of their own. In other words, they can
speak and they can hear. As a proof that the waters can
hear, we find that at the time of creation, God spoke to
the waters on two occasions and they responded promptly.

"And God said, Let the waters under the heaven be

gathered together unto one place, and let the dry land appear: and it was so... And God said, Let the waters bring forth abundantly the moving creature that hath life, and fowl that may fly above the earth in the open firmament of heaven. And God created great whales, and every living creature that moveth, which the waters brought forth abundantly, after their kind, and every winged fowl after his kind: and God saw that it was good." (Genesis 1:9-20,21).

Also, in the New Testament, we find Jesus commanding the sea to be still and it was so. Mark 4:35-39 says,

"On the same day, when evening had come, He said to them, "Let us cross over to the other side." Now when they had left the multitude, they took Him along in the boat as He was. And other little boats were also with Him. And a great windstorm arose, and the waves beat into the boat, so that it was already filling. But He was in the stern, asleep on a pillow. And they awoke Him and said to Him, "Teacher, do You not care that we are perishing?" Then He arose and rebuked the wind, and said to the sea, "Peace, be still!" And the wind ceased and there was a great calm."

I like the way that the Lord has recorded this passage for us. Jesus "rebuked" the wind, as one would do to a naughty child throwing tantrums, and it promptly obeyed. This shows us that regardless of the magnitude or multitude of powers controlling the seas, we can speak to them and they will instantly obey. More of this shall be explored later on.

As I mentioned at the beginning of this point, not only

can the waters hear, but they can also speak. This is the more reason why we need to speak often to them to counter their often negative utterances to our individual lives, communities and churches. Isaiah 23:4-5 says,

"Be ashamed, O Sidon; For the sea has spoken, the strength of the sea, saying, "I do not labor, nor bring forth children; Neither do I rear young men, Nor bring up virgins." When the report reaches Egypt, they also will be in agony at the report of Tyre."

Here, we find "the strength of the sea" or the powers of the sea declaring barrenness all over the land. As I have already stated, most of the times, it's negative declarations that proceed from the waters into our world – and it is up to us as believers to ensure that the demonic and destructive utterances and influences from the depths of the waters do not have a hold on our lives, churches and communities. We already have this unfailing promise that:

"The Lord will utterly destroy the tongue of the Sea of Egypt; With His mighty wind He will shake His fist over the River, and strike it in the seven streams, and make men cross over dry-shod." (Isaiah 11:15).

All we need to do therefore is to deploy our authority to gain the upper hand over the enemy.

5. Waters have healing essences.

Now, you may consider this to be ironic or contradictory, considering all the other negative things that have been said about the waters. But the truth is that as the first point above indicates and as we can confirm from Genesis 1, God never intended the waters to the habitations of evil and evil influences. God made everything to be for the good of man. Sadly, the invasion of the devil and his fallen angels, as well as the decision of man to hearken to the tempter's voice in the garden, gave the enemy some leverage to pervert many of the things that God had meant for man's good. Yet, God remains the supreme ruler of the universe and whenever He desires, He can make any of the elements which the enemy has invaded and perverted to be used for the original purpose for which He created them.

Again, having become heirs of God, believers equally have the authority to dominate the waters and convert them to God's purpose. This is why we find that many times waters were used to signify glorious blessings to the people of God and were equally used for healing purposes. I will be showing you later on additional instances of where believers exercised their dominion over the waters. But for now, let me show you some great healing and transforming benefits we can derive from waters if we can take our authority over them.Revelation 22:1-2 tells us of the great positive powers of waters:

> *"And he showed me a pure river of water of life, clear as crystal, proceeding from the throne of God and of the Lamb. In the middle of its street, and on either side of the river, was the tree of life, which bore twelve fruits, each tree yielding its fruit every month. The leaves of the tree were for the healing of the nations."*

We find here that it is this glorious river that supplies the nutrients that nourish and sustain the tree of life whose leaves are for the healing of the nations. Moreover, right here on earth, there have been several instances of where waters were used for healing. In 2 Kings 5:10-14, we read of the miraculous healing of Namaan, as he obeyed the instruction of Prophet Elisha. Also, in In John 9:6-7, we read of Jesus asking a blind man to go wash off the clay He had made and applied on his eyes in the pool of Siloam. And the man was healed as he obeyed. Again in John 5, we read of the pool of water which an angel came to trouble, and thereafter bringing healing to anyone who first stepped into it.

What I want you to observe in these different instances is the intervention of the divine upon the waters before they were converted to sources of healing. In some of the instances, we have the word of power being sent in advance to the waters, and in another instance, we find an angel having to come down to touch the water. What this means is that the waters can be of massive benefits to the people of God if we can fully understand the diverse deposits of riches, as well as the massive possibilities of healings and breakthroughs that God has put into them for our advantage.

CHAPTER SEVEN

MARINE POWERS AND THE LAST DAY CHURCH

I have decided to give special attention to this topic because so much ignorance and confusion persists among believers concerning the activities of marine powers in the world and in the church, especially in these last days. As a pastor who constantly interacts with church people from different denominations, I have observed that while believers seem to have much understanding about the earth and the heavens, including how to subdue the principalities and powers in high places, we have very little insight about the waters. Yet, this is the last day enemy and a lot of havoc is already being wreaked on our churches because of our ignorance.

Let me show you something interesting before we move on. In Mark 4:35, which we read earlier, we find Jesus telling the disciples that there was a need to cross over to the other side of the sea. In obedience, the disciples got into a boat and together with Jesus headed for their destination. However, shortly after they departed, something important happened: "And a great windstorm arose, and the waves beat into the boat, so that it was already filling.

> *But He was in the stern, asleep on a pillow. And they awoke Him and said to Him, "Teacher, do You not care that we are perishing?" (verses 37-38).*

You may consider the sudden rage of the sea here to be just a normal coincidence, until you fast-forward your reading to the next chapter. Mark 5:1-10 reads:

> *"Then they came to the other side of the sea, to the country of the Gadarenes. And when He had come out of the boat, immediately there met Him out of the tombs a man with an unclean spirit, who had his dwelling among the tombs; and no one could bind him, not even with chains, because he had often been bound with shackles and chains. And the chains had been pulled apart by him, and the shackles broken in pieces; neither could anyone tame him. And always, night and day, he was in the mountains and in the tombs, crying out and cutting himself with stones. When he saw Jesus from afar, he ran and worshiped Him. And he cried out with a loud voice and said, "What have I to do with You, Jesus, Son of the Most High God? I implore You by God that You do not torment me." For He said to him, "Come out of the man, unclean spirit!" Then He asked him, "What is your name?" And he answered, saying, "My name is Legion; for we are many." Also he begged Him earnestly that He would not send them out of the country."*

So, here it begins to get clearer. On the other side of the sea, where Jesus was going, a great miracle of deliverance was to occur. A man, whose destiny had been overturned and whose body had become a lair for multitudes of demons from the marine kingdom, was on the other side, desperately in need of freedom. Indeed, if until now, you still hadn't believed in the existence and viciousness of marine powers, I think this event should begin to make you have a rethink. These powers that controlled the country of the Gadarenes had seen Jesus coming and knew what was in store for them (You would see that it was immediately He arrived that the man from the tomb came to meet Him – as if they had been anxiously waiting!). Thus, they waged a fierce battle, which manifested in the storms. And so severe was the battle that the disciples, most of who were experienced fishermen and had encountered many waves before, became so powerless and we are told that the enemies seemed to have begun to conquer as the boat was already being filled with water, in preparation for capsizing. But just then the disciples took a drastic action that turned everything around.

I have referred to this story, first, to make you see that the influence of marine powers is real; and more importantly to make you see the link between what happened then and what the church is currently facing. We are living in a time which many in the past had prophesied to be a time of great awakening for the church and an unprecedented harvest of souls into the Kingdom of God. Like the declaration of Jesus, this time was supposed to be a time when the church would cross over to the next level of victory, dominion and spectacular move of the power and glory of God. But, looking at the state of many of our churches today, it is obvious that a demonic hijacking has occurred through the marine kingdom and the boat of the church is getting filled and almost capsizing under the weight of horrible scandals, backsliding and apostasy. And this, more than any other time in history, is the time believers, like the disciples, need to act, so that the counsel of God for us will prevail.

A UNIVERSAL MALADY

Two major demonic influences dominate today's world – sexual perversion and craze for wealth – and both are traced to the same source. Revelation 17:1-5 says,

"Then one of the seven angels who had the seven bowls came and talked with me, saying to me, "Come, I will show you the judgment of the great harlot who sits on many waters, with whom the kings of the earth committed fornication, and the inhabitants of the earth were made drunk with the wine of her fornication." So he carried me away in the Spirit into the wilderness. And I saw a woman sitting on a scarlet beast which was full of names of blasphemy, having seven heads and ten horns. The woman was arrayed in purple and scarlet, and adorned with gold and precious stones and pearls, having in her hand a golden cup full of abominations and the filthiness of her fornication. And on her forehead a name was written: MYSTERY, BABYLON THE GREAT, THE MOTHER OF HARLOTS AND OF THE ABOMINATIONS OF THE EARTH."

You will find that the three prominent things mentioned about this woman who "sits on" or controls many of the waters of the world are: her sophistication, her riches and her expertise at sexual perversion. Especially, with regards to her fornication, it is stated that while the leaders of the earth entered into covenants with her by sleeping with her directly, the other inhabitants of the earth had their fill of the wine or her fornication. Wine here indicates intoxicating pleasure; and when there is intoxication, both discretion and inhibition are lost.

Maybe now you can understand why glorification of sexual immorality pervades every segment of the modern world. The marine powers have infiltrated every facet of our world – from the fashion industry to the movie industry to the music industry, to advertising, to sports, to journalism, to government and even to areas that ordinarily should have no business with sexual perversion. Everywhere you turn it's the same wine of perversion that is being drunk by the young and the old, the male and the female, from one country to another. It has taken over our television. Almost everything on the TV these days is about lust. There are even programs dedicated to voyeurism – programs where you can watch people disrobe themselves or others and have sex to gain popularity or attract viewership for the debauched producers.

Our streets and everywhere have been taken over by these powers, and our young ones are not exempted. If you don't talk about sex these days, the world sees you as an archaic person.

Now, the most worrisome part of it all is that all these infiltrations are being done with the subtlety and sophistication that marine powers are known for. They present sexual immorality as the in-thing and promote it under the guise of liberation, female empowerment or simply celebration of the body. The most important word in the world of fashion today is to appear "sexy", which in its true sense means "looking like you want to have sex" or "looking in a way to stimulate sexual desire in the opposite gender." But the word continues to be used and promoted as if the meaning is totally normal.

The modus operandi of the marine powers in the world is simple. What they do is select a few individuals (mostly so-called celebrities) who are willing to sell their souls for money and they begin to use them to push the idea that sexual perversion is normal, natural or liberating. They slot them into movie roles or into some other influential places. They use them to promote the immorality trend, message and industry in such a way that almost everyone would get involved. In fact, just about a year ago, a popular female celebrity was said to have "broken the Internet" as multitudes from all over the world flocked to the Internet to catch a glimpse of her naked body.

This is the same trend that is being spread to young girls and women in the world. And the male gender have their significant share of this, though the marine world seems to have a special preference for females, perhaps because the overall head, as we have read in Revelation, is a female form. This is also the case with the pornography industry and adultery websites which continue to grow so massively that almost everyone thinks it's the appropriate thing to indulge in. This is the intoxicating wine of fornication that the entire earth is said to be drunk with.

One distinguishing trait of marine forces, as opposed to other evil strongholds in the universe, is their stupendous wealth. This is why Revelation 17:4 says

> *"The woman was arrayed in purple and scarlet, and adorned with gold and precious stones and pearls..."* *Ezekiel 28:4 also says of her, "With your wisdom and your understanding, you have gained riches for yourself, and gathered gold and silver into your treasuries; by your great wisdom in trade you have increased your riches, and your heart is lifted up because of your riches."*

The sex industry is one that rewards handsomely, so as to keep its captives perpetually bound and to draw multitudes of others into it. "Sex sells" is a popular slogan in the media and entertainment industries. Most of those sponsoring the sex industry or are promoting it appear to be so rich, powerful and influential in society. And these are the baits that keep more and more people attracted to this alluring but highly destructive world of marine kingdom influence.

THE CHURCH ANGLE

Unfortunately, the church that is supposed to be the salt and light of the world, whose major preoccupation should be depopulating the kingdom of darkness and populating the kingdom of God, especially in these last days, has itself become deeply enmeshed in the corrupting influences of the powers of the marine kingdom. The same appealing baits of subtlety, sophistication, wealth, popularity, power and influence that are being used to manipulate the outside world are what the marine powers are using to infiltrate the church today, with the additional twist of false spiritual gifts manifesting alongside massive immorality and perversion. This way, many Christians, including believers who had once been on fire for God have been destroyed both spiritually and physically.

Revelation 17:6 says of the influence of the marine power on the last day church: "I saw the woman, drunk with the blood of the saints and with the blood of the martyrs of Jesus. And when I saw her, I marveled with great amazement." I pray that your blood will not be part of that being drunk by the marine forces in these last days in Jesus' name. And it is for this reason that we must be aware and vigilant, so we don't get sucked in by the enticing pull of the woman sitting on the waters and her multitudes of agents that have been assigned against the church in this end time.

The method of operation of the marine kingdom against the church is in different forms. To start with, there are so-called churches that have been set up by agents of the marine kingdom themselves, with the goal of initiating multitudes into the marine world under the guise of worshipping God. For the discerning, it is not very difficult to identify these denominations but unfortunately many so-called Christians are just so in name; they know nothing of the Scripture and thus it is so easy for them to be deceived by these agents of Satan.

I said it is not difficult for the discerning to spot these extensions of the marine kingdom because every true child of God knows the foundation of the true church as stated in 1 Timothy 2:19,

"Nevertheless the foundation of God standeth sure, having this seal, The Lord knoweth them that are his.

*And, Let every one that nameth the name of Christ
depart from iniquity." (KJV).*

It is the contrary however that is being preached and
practiced in these false churches. There is often no mention
of repentance from sin or emphasis on holy living. What
they often preach is that Christ has paid for all our sins
before we commit them and thus there is no need to be
"sin-conscious". Emphasis is thus more on prosperity and
motivational sermons.

Naturally therefore the works of the flesh or, more
specifically, the lust of the flesh, which is the hallmark of
the marine kingdom, is the order of the day in these
churches. It becomes evident right from the dressing
pattern that is encouraged from the pulpit to the pew,
from the workers to the members – dressing that is
intended to arouse lustful desires. They hide the real
motive behind this or the effect thereof by pretending that
it doesn't matter, after all, "God is not interested in the
outward but the inward."

Where the complication lies for many and why the
undiscerning easily fall prey to these gatherings is that not
only do they seem to do well, with the members seemingly
prospering financially, but false gifts of the spirit often
manifest significantly. It could be in form of teaching –
where the minister seems to be eloquent with deep
knowledge of the Bible (which of course is interpreted in
such a way as to excite and not to convict, rebuke or
purify), healings and deliverances and most importantly
prophecy and revelation. Ezekiel 28:3 specifically mentions
this:

"Behold, you are wiser than Daniel! There is no secret that can be hidden from you!"

It thus becomes so easy for the gullible to be attracted to the lying wonders of these churches and the number of crowd and influence they have at their disposal.

But it is not only ordinary churchgoers who are deceived by the gimmicks of these marine centers. This brings us to another level of infiltration. As it happens in the world, sometimes some churches that were founded on the truth soon start getting attracted to the success of the marine churches. Consequently, some of the leaders and founders of these young churches in a bid to know the secrets of the success of the marine centers get in touch with the false pastors and form alliances. Such alliances may include going to the sea to receive power from the marine powers and sometimes they have sex with agents of the marine kingdom as in Revelation 17:1-2 who will empower the minister. And all he or she needs to constantly renew the power is to indulge in sexual perversion in the church. Thus, for power and prosperity, these ministers sell their souls and congregations.

The third form of infiltration is sending people possessed of the marine spirits into holiness churches to secretly and systematically seduce the ministers and members into sexual immorality; or simply introduce worldliness in dressing and worship and thus weaken or kill the church completely. These agents of the marine world sometimes infiltrate the workforce and spread the seeds of carnality and sexual immorality around. Where the challenge sometimes lies is that some of these people may be specially talented in one area of work or the other, or they may be influential in the church; and this sometimes makes the ministers in charge turn a blind eye, or treat their behaviors lightly by saying "judge not" or that "nobody is perfect".

This way, the enemy soon totally corrupts the church with worldliness, immorality and carnality and the glory of God gradually departs, until the church becomes spiritually dead. It is through this means that many mighty servants of God have been made useless and many churches that were once vibrant for real righteousness and the power of God have been reduced to mere entertainment centers. This was why Paul chastised the Corinthian church, saying:

"It is actually reported that there is sexual immorality among you… And you are puffed up, and have not rather mourned, that he who has done this deed might be taken away from among you… Your glorying is not good. Do you not know that a little leaven leavens the whole lump? Therefore purge out the old leaven, that you may be a new lump, since you truly are unleavened. For indeed Christ, our Passover, was sacrificed for us. Therefore let us keep the feast, not with old leaven, nor with the leaven of malice and wickedness, but with the unleavened bread of sincerity and truth" (1 Corinthians 5:1-8).

The church definitely has lot of work to do in these end times, if the forces of darkness from the marine kingdom will not prevail against it. Almost every day, we hear depressing reports of ministers of God and workers in the church being involved in all sorts of sex scandals, ranging from fornication and adultery to pornography and homosexuality. If we do not realize now that we are in a fierce battle and make every effort to use the weapons that

God has given us to prevail, then we may wake up when too much damage has been done. Strategies for our victory will form part of the next chapter.

CHAPTER EIGHT

DOMINION OVER THE WATERS AND THE MARINE KINGDOM

E ven though so much has been said about the powers and potentials of the sea, we still must know that man has been given dominion over it and all that's in it. For believers especially, we truly have nothing to worry about but to be glad that the Lord has made the waters and its numerous treasures and potentials for our benefits. All that we need is to believe God's word and assume the rightful position of authority that God has given to us.

The first thing I need to emphasize here is that we need not be afraid of the waters or their powers. Everything that God has made, including the waters, naturally succumbs to His order and authority. And since God has given us dominion over all the works of His hands, the waters will submit to us, if we do not magnify their powers above the word of God. In Psalm 29:3, we are told:

"The voice of the Lord is over the waters; The God of glory thunders; the Lord is over many waters. The voice of the Lord is powerful; the voice of the Lord is full of majesty."

The voice of the Lord being over the waters means that He has dominion over the waters and they are subject to His commands. Proverbs 21:1 is even more direct in describing God's power over the waters,

"The king's heart is in the hand of the LORD, like the rivers of water; He turns it wherever He wishes."

BELIEVERS' AUTHORITY OVER THE SEA

But as I have stated before, it is not only the voice of the Almighty God that the waters respond to; they also recognize and obey the commands of children of God. Jonathan Edwards, in his book, *Power of God* makes us understand how the dominion of God influences our dominion as believers. According to him: "Thus it is that souls espoused to Christ must reign over the world, because Christ reigns over the world...Because Jesus Christ is possessor of heaven, earth and sea, sun, moon and stars, so believers must be possessors of heaven, earth and sea, sun moon and stars too."

With specific reference to the sea, Jesus demonstrated his dominion over it when He commanded it to be still and it obeyed. However we have a more symbolic demonstration of this authority in His walking on the sea in Matthew 14:22-23:

"Immediately Jesus made His disciples get into the boat and go before Him to the other side, while He sent the multitudes away. And when He had sent the multitudes away, He went up on the mountain by Himself to pray. Now when evening came, He was alone there. But the boat was now in the middle of the sea, tossed by the waves, for the wind was contrary. Now in the fourth watch of the night Jesus went to them, walking on the sea. And when the disciples saw Him walking on the sea, they were troubled, saying, "It is a ghost!" And they cried out for fear.

But immediately Jesus spoke to them, saying, "Be of good cheer! It is I; do not be afraid. And Peter answered Him and said, "Lord, if it is You, command me to come to You on the water." So He said, "Come." And when Peter had come down out of the boat, he walked on the water to go to Jesus."

For the first time in history here, we have men walking on the sea. Christ did it first, to demonstrate His dominion over the powers of the sea, but He also demonstrated that through the power of His word, the same authority has been conferred on believers by asking Peter to do what He was doing and Peter successfully did!

The message, in all these, as I have noted before, is that whatever we may have heard or read about the sea or marine powers shouldn't cause us to panic or make us consider them invincible. Every knee must bow at the mention of the name of Jesus, whether it is on earth or in the sea (Philippians 2:9-10).

Indeed, a full realization of our dominion over the sea

would make us focus more on getting its numerous benefits and converting it to our advantage. This way, the healing powers, the treasures and the resources in the sea can be turned to us, and we can make the sea work for us as a servant, rather than working against us. Many saints of old demonstrated this and we can learn from them.

We already know about Moses, how after receiving the word from the Lord turned the waters of Egypt into blood. We also have the same Moses parting the Red Sea for the people of God to cross over to the other side. This shows that believers have the authority to break through any difficulty or opposition that wants to prevent them from moving to the next level of their destinies and getting to their Promised Land.

We also read in Joshua 4:13, how God told Joshua,

> *"And it shall come to pass, as soon as the soles of the feet of the priests who bear the ark of the Lord, the Lord of all the earth, shall rest in the waters of the Jordan, that the waters of the Jordan shall be cut off, the waters that come down from upstream, and they shall stand as a heap."*

And of course, it happened as the Lord had said.

Interestingly, we find Jesus Christ, as well as believers of old, also showing us what real possession of something for our benefit and for the glory of God looks like. If you look at the Gospels closely, you would find that many of Christ's ministrations were done around rivers, in fulfillment of Isaiah's prophecy in Isaiah 9:1. Also in the Early Church, we find instances of believers converting places around waters to prayer centers (See Act 16:13; 20:

36-38 for examples).

Earlier on in the Old Testament, we find great men of God like Elijah and Elisha doing a similar thing. In fact, it was not by accident that the mantle of Elijah fell on Elisha by the river of Jordan. It was simply because Elijah had always prayed near the river. So the falling of the mantle there was symbolic of the transfer of the ministry. This was why Naaman was directed by Elisha to the same river to bathe.

In the Psalms, we find the psalmist in Psalm 137:1-3 saying that the people of God wept by the rivers of Babylon when they remembered Zion. Why was this? It was because they had always seen their prophets praying by the riverside. An example was Ezekiel who went to people living by the rivers of Chebar and waited on the Lord for seven days. After the seven days, the word of the Lord came to him. Right at that river, God spoke to him to make him a watchman. (See Ezekiel 1:3; 3: 15-17).

What this means for us is that we must learn to take possession of every part of the universe which the Lord has committed to our hands and reap the benefits thereby; no part must be ceded to the forces of darkness or even for only unbelievers to explore. It is not meet to give the children's bread to dogs!

COMBATTING AND EXPELLING MARINE INFLUENCES IN THE CHURCH

Having seen that dominion over the waters is our birthright as children of God and that the victory has been won for us by Christ, we now return to the burning issue in these last days – the influence of marine powers in the church of God. Again, as we consider this, let us realize that Christ who is the Head of the church is also very much concerned about the state of things; so we must know that we are not alone in winning the victory. The same Revelation 17 that talks about the devastations caused on the church by the woman sitting on the waters, also makes us to know that God is interested in avenging His people by crushing this ruler of the marine kingdom, which Ezekiel describes as a very arrogant dragon that tries to equate itself with God (see Ezekiel 28).

In Revelation 17:1, the Scripture says, "Then one of the seven angels who had the seven bowls came and talked with me, saying to me, "Come, I will show you the judgment of the great harlot who sits on many waters…" So, we know that the judgment of God is sure on this power. However, for victory to be ours as a church, we have our roles to play. These include:

1. Discernment and watchfulness.

These two must go together. Discernment comes in two ways – discernment as to understanding the peculiarity of the times in which we live (like the children of Issachar in 1 Chronicles 12:32) and also be able to discern what kind of spirit is manifesting in our churches at every point in time. Both forms of discernment will naturally require us to be watchful, so we are not caught unawares by the subtlety of marine spirits.

For discernment of the times, we already have understanding of that, as much as been said about that here. The times are perilous. The battle is fiercer now that the coming of

Christ is nearer and the enemy is more desperate than ever to completely paralyze the church, especially through the cunning infiltration and deception of marine spirits. They are everywhere and EVERY living church is a target.

As for discernment of spirits, this is more crucial and more demanding. It requires that the minister himself understand that he is on a battlefield and thus must be on fire for God every time, so as to be sensitive to the promptings of the Holy Spirit. Not every gifted preacher, singer, prophesier, teacher or healer is a child of God. It is not every charismatic, crowd-pulling preacher that we have to partner with or invite to minister in our church. We must be discerning in the spirit and watch out for the red signals of elevating miracles and excitement above the true word of God.

As incredible as it may sound, some seemingly zealous religious people are operating under the influence of marine spirits and are just using whatever else they are doing in the church as a smokescreen to perpetrate their evil. We have a good example of how this works in Acts 16:16-18,

> *"Now it happened, as we went to prayer, that a certain slave girl possessed with a spirit of divination met us, who brought her masters much profit by fortune-telling. This girl followed Paul and us, and cried out, saying, "These men are the servants of the Most High God, who proclaim to us the way of salvation." And this she did for many days. But Paul, greatly annoyed, turned and said to the spirit, "I command you in the name of Jesus Christ to come out of her." And he came out that very hour."*

An undiscerning minister would have seen this girl to be so zealous for God and a potential assistant in the ministry. But Paul knew better that she was operating under a marine spirit and was simply looking for a way to infiltrate the ranks of the apostles to cause havoc. This is how many seemingly zealous and gifted corrupters have been recruited into the workforce of many churches and thus leading to destruction from within. I pray you will be vigilant in Jesus' name.

Our discernment will also make us to watch against any traces of worldliness in comportment, dressing and worship in the church. Every appearance of sensuality in speech, behavior and dressing, as well as songs whose lyrics, beats and rhythms are alien to the people of God and capable of stirring up lust must be rejected, regardless of protestations from the undiscerning.

2. Commitment to biblical doctrines at all times

One of the ways of knowing marine churches or churches that are already being infiltrated by marine influences is the way they handle the word of God and what areas of the Scripture they love to emphasize. 1 Timothy 4:1 says,

"Now the Spirit expressly says that in latter times some will depart from the faith, giving heed to deceiving spirits and doctrines of demons." Again, Paul tells Timothy in 2 Timothy 4:1-4, "I charge you therefore before God and the Lord Jesus Christ, who will judge the living and the dead at His appearing and His kingdom: Preach the word! Be ready in season and out of season. Convince, rebuke, exhort, with all longsuffering and teaching. For the time will come when they will not

endure sound doctrine, but according to their own desires, because they have itching ears, they will heap up for themselves teachers; and they will turn their ears away from the truth, and be turned aside to fables."

This is what is happening today in many churches. People only want to hear exciting and motivational messages - messages that thrill the flesh but do nothing to transform the spirit. This makes such places fertile breeding grounds for marine spirits. Satanic spirits cannot tolerate a place where the true gospel on holiness and righteousness is regularly emphasized. They will either do all they can to derail the minister or they themselves flee. Light and darkness never mingle!

Thus, the word of God on holiness and righteous living must be upheld at every time in our churches. Cardinal doctrines of the Bible such as the depravity of the natural man, the destructive nature of sin, the need for salvation and genuine repentance, conditional security through the grace of God, the reality of heaven and hell, the rapture and so on, must remain priorities in our churches. We must not be so advanced that we neglect these teachings for the bandwagon of prosperity and mere motivation, which is one of the easiest ways through which marine spirits penetrate.

And not only must we preach, we must be seen to practice what we preach and ensure those around us do same. There must not be room for compromise. Holiness must be our watchword in all that we do and it's the same lifestyle of holiness we must encourage at all times in our congregation.

3. Prayer

The vultures of the marine kingdom can only gather where they find a church that has become a carcass through prayerlessness. A church where the fire of prayer is either non-existent or has been extinguished is a convenient breeding ground for marine spirits or any other demonic power for that matter. This brings to mind the instruction that God gave the children of Israel concerning their place of worship:

> *"And the fire on the altar shall be kept burning on it; it shall not be put out...A fire shall always be burning on the altar; it shall never go out." (Leviticus 6:12-13).*

We must keep the fire of prayer burning, regardless of every attempt to distract us. Of course, there will be distractions. Satan and his agents will manipulate events and instigate people to ensure that we neglect prayer. He will do all he can to ensure that we are busy with every other thing except prayer – because he knows that any religious activity we engage in without the involvement of the Spirit of God and prayer is nothing but mere entertainment. This was why the apostles refused to be distracted when the issue of food serving arose in the Early Church. They clearly declared,

> *"It is not desirable that we should leave the word of God and serve tables. Therefore, brethren, seek out from among you seven men of good reputation, full of the Holy Spirit and wisdom, whom we may appoint over this business; but we will give ourselves continually to prayer and to the ministry of the word" (Acts 6:2-4).*

Thank God they were vigilant enough not to allow the manipulation of the enemy to make them abandon prayer. We too must continually give ourselves to the different forms of prayer to wage war against the incursion, influence or activities of marine powers in our congregations. I said "different forms of prayer" because there are prayers of defense and there are prayers of attack. In other words, there are prayers we pray to fortify our churches with the blood of the Lamb against every arrow from the marine kingdom (Revelation 12:11); and there are prayers we pray when we notice any indication that a negative influence is creeping in or is observed in any member of the congregation.

We must learn to command the waters and declare God's word. As we have been instructed in Ezekiel 29:2-3, we must learn to command the gates of the waters to be opened and command the fire of God to destroy the palace of the evil one, where any attack or monitoring from the enemy may be coming from. We must deal with the dragon in the midst of the river. We must bind and disarm the dragon in the water. As often as possible, we must combine our prayers with fasting. Above all, let's remember that Christ has given us the victory on the cross already; ours is to claim and activate what has been done.

4. Discipline

We cannot effectively discuss strategies to deal with the influence of marine spirits without including this crucial aspect. In actual fact, the reason the enemy has succeeded in sowing and spreading his influence in many churches is because the modern-day church seems so weak in this important area of church administration. It is natural – a place where there are no boundaries is a place where anything goes!

Discipline is an indispensable deterrent or defense mechanism against disorder and destruction. No child ever grows up without discipline and leads a responsible life. No trainee ever becomes an expert without discipline. Even God in dealing with every one of His children takes discipline as a priority. Hebrews 12:6-8 says,

> *"For whom the Lord loves He chastens, and scourges every son whom He receives." If you endure chastening, God deals with you as with sons; for what son is there whom a father does not chasten? But if you are without chastening, of which all have become partakers, then you are illegitimate and not sons."*

What we however find in many of our churches today and which the powers of darkness and marine spirits, in particular, take advantage of is our seeming inability or unwillingness to rebuke or discipline erring members or workers. We don't want to offend or hurt anyone and we want a church that will remain of fire for God. It is like a doctor who wants people to remain healthy but doesn't want them to go through the pains of injection and surgery or the inconveniences of pills. It's impossible!

It is this indulgent attitude towards sin and the appearances of sin in the church that makes the activities of marine spirits to spread quickly among a congregation. This was the major reason Paul the Apostle was aggrieved with the Corinthian church and he wondered how they expected to have a healthy and vibrant church when they were busy pampering the cancer of sin, rather than cutting it off immediately with decisive action. To quote the passage we read earlier:

> *"Your glorying is not good. Do you not know that a little leaven leavens the whole lump?" (1 Corinthians 5:6).*

Well, that's exactly how many of our churches have become leavened with the leaven of lust and worldliness. We keep on glorying about population, prosperity and signs and wonders, while the enemies keep rejoicing that all we are doing is for their own benefit as more and more people are being lured to hell right under our watch. I pray that the Lord will jolt us to make amends in Jesus' name.

Once again, let's be reminded that discipline is one of the mandates we have been given as ministers of the gospel, and it is one of the most powerful strategies to keep our churches from being overrun by the "little foxes" of lust, sexual immorality, worldliness and carnality. Here is 2 Timothy 4:1-2 again,

> *"I charge you therefore before God and the Lord Jesus Christ, who will judge the living and the dead at His appearing and His kingdom: Preach the word! Be ready in season and out of season. Convince, REBUKE, exhort, with all longsuffering and teaching."*

It must be added though that another major reason that some ministers find it hard to enforce discipline in their churches is because they themselves are not living a transparent, holy life. And so they worry that they too might be exposed if they discipline others; or they worry that if they are hard on erring members, then they will get a similar treatment when they themselves are eventually caught. This is why a minister who has been called by God to handle the important but delicate ministry of pastoring must keep himself blameless through the grace of God and watchfulness at all times.

May victory continue to be ours as we obey the Lord in Jesus' name.

PART 3

TAKE CHARGE, RULE THE HEAVENS

CHAPTER NINE

GLORIES OF THE HEAVENS

Having taken a spiritual exploration of the worlds beneath and around us, we now come to the one above us. We come to the world of the planetary forces and the atmospheric elements – the world of the skies, the sun, the moon, the stars and the weather.

This may as well be the most important of the worlds, after all, as the NewScientist magazine reported in a recent edition: "We are creatures of the air more than any other of the classical elements. Though we walk on solid ground and take the occasional dip in the sea, we are always in intimate contact with the atmosphere – immersed in it, sucking it in by the lungful to stay alive, and subject to the whims of its weather."

The above is absolutely true; but there is even much more to be noted. The movements and activities of the heavenly bodies not only dictate the weather conditions on earth, but they also regulate the course of our days, by controlling when we sleep and when we wake up to go about our daily activities (night and day). They determine our various seasons – summer, winter, fall, autumn and so on.

Moreover, the heavens harbor much more than the familiar atmospheric attractions that we see from time to time, and this means that they certainly do more than just affect our days, weathers or seasons. To quote the NewScientist again: "Despite this intimacy [which we think we have with the heavens], the atmosphere has kept many secrets from us. The air is home to eerie lights and portentous glows, shimmering wisps of ice on the edge of space and invisible tides. There is even life up among the clouds…"

This exactly is the truth we shall be exploring here. The fact is that while the "life up among the clouds" which the magazine referred to are, by its explanation, limited to just bacteria and fungi, which are always "munching on chemicals", the Bible confirms to us that there are creatures up there that can actually munch lives and crunch destinies; there are forces up there that constantly monitor the earth, decide the course of events in the world and control people's minds and behaviors. Let's delve deeper into this reality.

POWERS OF THE AIR

For starters, Ephesians 2:1-2 reveals to us that the reason we have so much disobedience and rebellion against the word of God in families, institutions, communities and even churches today is because of the activities of the forces of the air. It says, "And you He made alive, who were dead in trespasses and sins, in which you once walked according to the course of this world, according to the prince of the power of the air, the spirit who now works in the sons of disobedience."

We are also told in Daniel 10 that nations and communities have demonic forces attached to them by Satan. Their purpose is to seek to influence the course of events in these nations and frustrate the will of God for them. They try to achieve these by making people rebel against God, by stirring up calamities and bloodshed, by waging war against the church of God and by preventing answers to prayers. In the same Daniel 10, references are made to the Prince of the nation of Persia (verses 12-13) and the Prince of Greece (verse 20), which were the ruling powers of the airs in these nations and which fought desperately to hinder Daniel's prayers. Paul the apostle added more details to this when he says:

> *"For we do not wrestle against flesh and blood, but against principalities, against powers, against the rulers of the darkness of this age, against spiritual hosts of wickedness in the heavenly places" (Ephesians 6:12).*

There is indeed wickedness in the heavenly places and because of the position of the heavens to the earth, the earth is usually the experimental laboratory and dumping ground for all sorts perversions and wickedness coming from the wicked forces above. Moreover, because the heavenly elements regulate days and nights on earth, it becomes so easy for demonic forces to manipulate each day and program multitudes of evils into it, so that as the day dawns, a fresh wave of calamities dawn with it. This is why Jesus says that sufficient unto the day is the evil thereof (Matthew 6:34).

This same programming can be done into the nights. In fact, the night time is often the time the demonic forces in the air and those on earth and in the sea mostly program their evils and unleash them on humanity. This is why the psalmist not only talks of the arrow that flies by day but also of the terror of the night (Psalm 91:5).

But it is not all gloomy about the heavens. Indeed, much more than the two other worlds that we have considered, the heavens contain the very Fountain of all blessings and blessedness; they harbor the Spring of all riches and richness, the very extent of which our minds can never ever fathom. An immediate indication of the immense blessings overflowing in the heavens is that it is from the same heavens that we get the rains and the dew that nourish the earth and rejuvenate the whole of nature, providing continual sustenance for man and beast.

It is from the same heavens that we get solar energy that powers many homes, industries and appliances. And it is from the same heavens that we get the electromagnetic spectrum (or radio waves) on which all of the gadgets and mechanisms with which we transmit and receive digital information globally depend. And much more than these, there are inexhaustible possibilities and wonders in the heavens that we can attract into our lives.

LEVELS OF HEAVENS

What I meant by the "Fountain of all blessings and blessedness" and "the Spring of all riches and richness" above is that, cheeringly and interestingly, it is in the same heavens that the Almighty God dwells. It is there that the holy angels, the heavenly hosts and all the saints who have gone before us dwell.

Does there seem to be a contradiction here? How can the wicked forces in the air and the holy God dwell in the same place? Don't worry, I'll explain. Did you notice that I have continued to use the word "heavens" and not just "heaven"? That is where the answer lies. Heavens have levels which are immeasurably far apart. As a proof of the levels of heavens, here is what Paul wrote: "It is doubtless not profitable for me to boast. I will come to visions and revelations of the Lord: I know a man in Christ who fourteen years ago—whether in the body I do not know, or whether out of the body I do not know, God knows— such a one was caught up to the third heaven. And I know such a man—whether in the body or out of the body I do not know, God knows— how he was caught up into Paradise and heard inexpressible words, which it is not lawful for a man to utter." (2 Corinthians 1:4).

Paul, here, mentions the "third heaven", which he calls paradise. This means that there are two heavens below this. Theologians generally agree that the first heaven is the atmosphere, right above the earth. The second heaven is the abode of the wicked demons in high places, the principalities that many worship in the name of worshipping the heavenly bodies. They are the vicious forces that launch continuous attacks against humanity and control the systems of the world. It was one of these that confronted Angel Gabriel while bringing the answer to Daniel's prayers in Daniel 10. So it is obvious that these forces have a lot of influence on the earth. They make or mar destinies; they can hinder prayers, cause delays, unleash mayhem and foresee what many on earth cannot see. They are the ones the Lord Jesus Christ mentioned in Matthew 24:29 that their power will be shaken.

More interestingly, far above where the wicked forces reside, the Almighty God reigns and rules in majesty. This is where Christ ascended to, and it is from here that He continually makes intercession for us so that the purpose of God for our lives will be fulfilled without being hijacked by the wicked ones.Ephesians 1:19-21 tells us:

> *"And what is the exceeding greatness of his power to us-ward who believe, according to the working of his mighty power, Which he wrought in Christ, when he raised him from the dead, and set him at his own right hand in the heavenly places, Far above all principality, and power, and might, and dominion, and every name that is named". Also in Ephesians 4:9, we are told, "Now this, "He ascended"—what does it mean but that He also first descended into the lower parts of the earth? He who descended is also the One who ascended far above all the heavens, that He might fill all things."*

WHAT'S THE MESSAGE?

Why am I telling you all this? It is to let you know, first of all, that regardless of all you may hear or read about the influence and wickedness of principalities and powers in the heavenly places, you have the One who is seated far above them on your side. And if you can be in accord and communion with Him, then no power in the universe can intimidate or conquer you.

Again, I'm telling you all of this so you can know that if you want to have true dominion in your life and over the world around you, you must know how to wage war in the heavens. It is also to let you know how much power the heavens wield over the earth and prove to you that if you can have power in the heavens, then you can influence a lot of issues concerning your life and the world around you.

You therefore need not worry about how many or how vicious the satanic forces in the universe are. In fact, and this should really bolster your faith, Christ has paid the price for your victory over the heavenly forces already. In doing this, he has disarmed them, so that you can be all that the Almighty God has purposed you to be without any unnecessary interference from the demonic hosts. Colossians 2:15 assures us, "Having disarmed principalities and powers, He made a public spectacle of them, triumphing over them in it."

This calls for rejoicing and demonstration of dominion by every believer over the heavens and thus over the events on earth. Sadly, however, as with the earth and the sea, believers don't wield as much power as they should over the heavens because we seem to have limited knowledge of the hustle-bustle of activities going on up there – and especially how these activities affect our lives on earth. In consideration of this reality, it is important we explore additional salient truths about the heavens so that we can have the dominion that God expects us to have.

CHAPTER TEN

BELIEVERS' VICTORY IN THE HEAVENLY PLACES

A ncient astrologers and philosophers all acknowledge the influential powers of planetary forces. They know, for example, that the stars have important information about individuals' lives and destinies encoded into them. This is why stargazing used to be a very common practice in many parts of the world. Both the heavenly forces and some people with special powers on earth (called wise men in the Bible), including Satan-empowered psychics and mediums, are able to study the stars to decode the destinies of individuals. They can also study other heavenly bodies to foretell events in the lives of individuals and communities – and this way, they can also exchange and manipulate people's destinies.

POWERS OF THE STARS

When Jesus Christ was born, for instance, some stargazers were able to decode that a very unusual child or, more precisely, a spectacular king had been born. Matthew 2:1-2 says,

> *"Now after Jesus was born in Bethlehem of Judea in the days of Herod the king, behold, wise men from the East came to Jerusalem, saying, "Where is He who has been born King of the Jews? For we have seen His star in the East and have come to worship Him."*

Well, while it is true that these wise men actually had good intentions, many of the other forces, especially the heavenly powers, who study the stars never have good intentions. Their primary purpose is to see how to thwart God's program for individuals, communities, churches and nations, by either triggering events that could sabotage the fulfillment of this program or they find a way to manipulate the individuals concerned to deviate from God's word and way and thus miss His purpose for them.

The first strategy is what we find in the declaration of Pharaoh in the Old Testament concerning Moses. At the time Moses was to be born, the principalities of the air had seen his destiny and thus incited Pharaoh to issue a decree to have all newborn male Hebrew children to be killed (Exodus 1:22). We find a similar approach in the case of Herod in the New Testament concerning Jesus Christ. As soon as Herod heard from the wise men that a king had been born, he was instigated by the demonic forces of the air to seek to kill the child. And so, he issued a decree that all male infants in Bethlehem and the surrounding communities must be killed (Matthew 2:16). In both instances, multitudes of lives were lost, simply because the enemy wanted to get rid of someone whose survival he knew would transform the course of history for good. The same still happens to this very day.

The second strategy that evil stargazers and powers of the air often use to truncate a glorious destiny does not require much explanation because we find glaring examples all through history and all around us. Many people with great prospects, gifts and abilities have become wasted and turned to nonentities or even prematurely killed through the power of sin and disobedience to God, as instigated by the powers of the air. I pray you don't become a victim yourself.

The message for us in this is that we must always be extra vigilant, so that the forces of the air will never be able to tamper with, exchange or totally ruin our destinies. We must continually preempt and frustrate, by fervent prayer and holy living, every device of the enemy against our destiny.

Job 5:12 says of the ability of God to defend our destiny:

"He frustrates the devices of the crafty, So that their hands cannot carry out their plans."

The kind of prayer that we pray to safeguard our destinies is not the ordinary kind of prayer; it must be prophetic battle prayer. But then, we cannot just settle for only defensive prayers when it comes to the stars. The fact is that we too can use the stars to work in our favor. We can declare to the stars to reject every negative pronouncement or programming that is being done against us.

Beyond that, we can actually use the stars to fight against every adversary of our progress and every contender with our destiny. An example of such was Sisera, the captain of the Canaanite army who fought against the Israelites. The Bible tells us how he was dealt with:

> *"They fought from the heavens; the stars from their courses fought against Sisera." (Judges 5:20).*

What happened here confirms the point that I have repeatedly made in this book – that the people of old seemed to know what to do with the elements of the universe far better than we do. Here, we are told that it was not only physical soldiers that were used to conquer Sisera; the hosts of heaven were also employed against him.

The second important lesson we must get from here is that battles on earth are best won when they're fought from heaven. Since the heavens rule the earth, it goes without saying that if we can have power over the heavens, then no battle on earth will be too difficult for us to crush. The spiritual controls the physical, and if we can have dominion in the spiritual world, then nothing can subdue us in the physical world.

POWERS OF THE SUN AND THE MOON

But it is not only the stars that harbor great potentials that we can either harness for our good or leave to the mercy of the wicked ones to manipulate against us. Both the sun and the moon are powerful elements of the universe. The ancient people knew about this. They knew the secret about these forces; that was why some went to the extreme length of worshipping them.

Just like the stars, the sun and the moon can be used to wreak havoc on humanity. This is why God promises the believer in Psalm 121:5-6,

> *"The sun shall not strike you by day, nor the moon by night."*

This means that the sun and the moon have the power to smite a person and the enemies have used this against many.

As I stated previously, it is because of this numerous potentials of the sun that has made many to turn it to an object of worship. Ironically, people who claim to be serving the living God sometimes engage in worshipping the sun and the stars. Ezekiel recorded his experience with such people:

> *"So He brought me into the inner court of the Lord's house; and there, at the door of the temple of the Lord, between the porch and the altar, were about twenty-five men with their backs toward the temple of the Lord and their faces toward the east, and they were worshiping the sun toward the east" (Ezekiel 8:16).*

That's what many so-called Christians do today. They come to church, but their faith is not rested in God. They still consult horoscopes, Ouija board, psychics, palm-readers, and stargazers. The end result of that is what God states in verse 18 of that same chapter: "Therefore I also will act in fury. My eye will not spare nor will I have pity; and though they cry in My ears with a loud voice, I will not hear them." This tells us that this is why answers to some prayers are delayed – because God knows that we have alternative sources of help.

The moon on its part has massive powers that can be used to alter people's states of mind. "Luna" is an ancient term for the moon. This is why people who had mental problems were often referred to as "lunatics" because it was believed that certain actions and movements of the moon can actually affect people's mental state.

Sadly with the penchant of modern scientists to explain away supernatural events, many beliefs about the moon are being dismissed. Yet none of the so-called knowledgeable scientists seems to be able to explain the reason for the alarming rise in the rate of depression, bipolar disorders and suicidal tendencies in modern times, despite availability of fun gadgets and entertainment platforms. This is a question that should continually ring in our minds whenever we are tempted to dismiss the potentials of the heavenly powers: Why is it that suicide rate continues to soar, despite the trappings of fun and luxury all around?

Companies all over the world continue to manufacture drugs that they think can combat the soaring scourge of depression and insanity everywhere, yet the situation continues to get worse. Recently, CDC's National Centre for Health Statistics reported that suicide rates in the United States are the highest they had been in three decades, increasing 24 per cent between 1999 and 2014. On the global scene, it is reported that in the last 45 years, suicide rates have increased by 60%. Psychologists, scientists and medical practitioners continue to scramble for explanations but they can't provide anything convincing. The more they explain, the more young people continue to create popular suicide sites and schemes, physically and online. Don't be deceived – satanic manipulation through the moon is real!

The more disturbing aspect is that even those of us who are Christians sometimes get carried away by medical and scientific explanations and we tend to rate them above God's word. Sometimes we have children battling depression, addictions and showing other strange symptoms and we erroneously buy the idea that they can be cured by drugs. The reality is that what science can't explain, the scriptures can. And we certainly need to be ahead of scientists in matters like this, because what these children require, most times, is not drugs but dominion over the forces of the air.

Here again, we have a great example from our Lord Jesus Christ:

> *"And when they were come to the multitude, there came to him a certain man, kneeling down to him, and saying, Lord, have mercy on my son: for he is lunatick, and sore vexed: for ofttimes he falleth into the fire, and oft into the water. And I brought him to thy disciples, and they could not cure him. Then Jesus answered and said, O faithless and perverse generation, how long shall I be with you? how long shall I suffer you? bring him hither to me. And Jesus rebuked the devil; and he departed out of him: and the child was cured from that very hour." (Matthew 17:14-18).*

I hope you observed the word there – lunatic. And did you observe both the action of the father of the boy and that of Jesus? The father claimed that the boy was lunatic and he did not think that the solution was in medicine; he knew that what the boy was contending with required a spiritual battle and he was desperate enough to seek Jesus to get the victory. And did you observe that Jesus did not send him to get drugs? He understood that it was indeed a demonic manipulation that required the word of authority from Him and thus requested that the boy be brought to Him. Most importantly, we realize that it was indeed a spirit that was behind the insanity.

Please, don't misunderstand me - I am not against use of medicines or using medicines to treat mental disorders where possible. But my point is that many mental, emotional and psychological maladies that we send to the medics are actually cases that should be brought to Jesus. No amount of medicines can cure manipulations from the forces of the air; we need to deploy the power and authority that we have, using the all-powerful name of JESUS!

CHAPTER ELEVEN

COMMANDING THE HEAVENS FOR OUR BENEFIT

Let me emphasize it again – the heavens certainly have powers and possibilities that God embedded in them, just as He did the earth and the sea. These powers are to be used for our benefit. They are to be deployed to assist in accomplishing God's purpose for our lives. A good way to do this is what we find in Exodus 10:21-23,

> *"Then the Lord said to Moses, "Stretch out your hand toward heaven, that there may be darkness over the land of Egypt, darkness which may even be felt." So Moses stretched out his hand toward heaven, and there was thick darkness in all the land of Egypt three days. They did not see one another; nor did anyone rise from his place for three days."*

It was the will of God for the Israelites to be delivered from the bondage of the Egyptians. And to achieve it,

Moses had to invoke the power of the heavens. He invoked continuous darkness upon the land of Egypt to break the hardened heart of Pharaoh. This is what God has given us the earth, the sea and the heavens to accomplish – to cooperate with us in the actualization of the purpose of our existence. And we must make use of this possibility; otherwise – as I have mentioned again and again – the evil ones who equally know how powerful these elements are can use them against us instead.

COMMAND, NOT WORSHIP!

Now, this equally must be emphasized - inasmuch as the heavenly bodies are powerful, they are not meant to be worshipped; they are meant to be commanded. You worship what you consider superior and these forces are not superior to us; they are meant to be our subjects. It is God, who has encoded their abilities into them, that deserves all our worship.

Knowing the tendency of man to misplace priorities – to ignore the substance while chasing the shadow - God has given us strict warnings on the worship of heavenly elements throughout the Scripture. The one in Deuteronomy 4:19 is particularly explicit:

> *"And take heed, lest you lift your eyes to heaven, and when you see the sun, the moon, and the stars, all the host of heaven, you feel driven to worship them and serve them, which the Lord your God has given to all the peoples under the whole heaven as a heritage."*

You see that? God has given us these elements as a heritage, not as spectacles to be worshipped. And for anyone who goes against this, either by direct worship of these forces or through more subtle means like horoscope, fortune-telling and the likes, the judgment of God is sure.

You may wonder why horoscope reading or consulting palm-readers or fortune-tellers count as worship of the heavens. It's simple. When you or someone else consults your "star" to know about your life, you are simply ascribing the power, authority and glory which belong to God alone to that medium; so beware! This is why God gave another strict warning on this in Deuteronomy 18:10-12 (KJV),

> *"There shall not be found among you any one that maketh his son or his daughter to pass through the fire, or that useth divination, or an observer of times, or an enchanter, or a witch, Or a charmer, or a consulter with familiar spirits, or a wizard, or a necromancer. For all that do these things are an abomination unto the Lord..."*

When God calls someone or a nation an abomination, then you can be sure that He will find a way to punish or wipe out such from His presence. He says in Deuteronomy 4:26 that all who will flout His instruction to flee from idolatry and worship of created things will be uprooted from the land of their inheritance and scattered to unknown places. And you can be sure that if God says He will do something, He certainly will.

There are many ways in which God scatters rebellious individuals and nations. It can be by catastrophes or natural disasters, such as earthquakes and the likes. It can also be through outbreak of war. In recent times, we have seen many nations, especially those known to be devoted to worshipping the moon, severely destabilized by war and disasters, with the citizens fleeing to other countries of the world.

So, once again – the heavens are our heritage and we must take dominion over them by commanding them to work in our favor. Since the heavens shape the course of events on earth then we must take hold of the heavens by prayers of faith and declarative statements. The heavens can hear, and since they are at our command, they will obey.

MODELS OF FAITH

I showed you before what Joshua did and since it's very relevant here, I will quote the passage again:

> *"Then Joshua spoke to the Lord in the day when the Lord delivered up the Amorites before the children of Israel, and he said in the sight of Israel: "Sun, stand still over Gibeon; And Moon, in the Valley of Aijalon." So the sun stood still, And the moon stopped, Till the people had revenge Upon their enemies. Is this not written in the Book of Jasher? So the sun stood still in the midst of heaven, and did not hasten to go down for about a whole day. And there has been no day like that, before it or after it, that the Lord heeded the voice of a man; for the Lord fought for Israel" (Joshua 10:12-14).*

Oh that God would raise men and women of faith like this among us again. Men and women who understand the full extent of their position, power and authority in Christ and can order the forces of nature to do their biddings to the glory of God! Isn't it amazing that the

Bible says that no one had ever done what Joshua did before? Where then did he get such courage and confidence to command the sun and the moon to alter their normal courses? First it was from the absolute confidence he had in the word of God. If you read earlier verses in that chapter, you would find that God had assured him that He had given the enemy nations to the Israelites to conquer. That was all that Joshua needed. Since God had said that the nation was theirs, then every other power, including the planetary forces, must bow! This was why it happened that when he saw the sun going down and the moon coming up when the word of God had not been fully fulfilled concerning Israel's victory, he had to order both elements to halt their movements!

I don't know if you are catching the Rhema in this exposition. When God promises or declares something for us, it doesn't mean that there would be nothing that would want to withstand or oppose the fulfillment. But it is left for us to either be intimidated or stand boldly on the immutability of the word of God and command every other power to bow. Let God be true and every other man or force in heaven, on earth or under the earth, be a liar.

The second source of inspiration for Joshua's unprecedented action was the experience he had had with his departed mentor, Moses. He certainly must have seen or heard about how he raised his hands to heaven and brought thick darkness upon the land of Egypt. He also must have seen how he brought water from the rock, as well as other wonders. And he decided to do same.

The challenge is upon us today. As the Scripture says,

"these things were written for our learning" (Romans 15:4).

There are many other examples of people who commanded the forces of nature and of the universe, which Joshua had no privilege of seeing because the Bible had not been written. But here we are, we have seen and heard of what God did though believers who dared to use their authority. I pray that we will do even better in Jesus' name.

We also have the powerful challenge from Elijah, who shut the heavens that there should be no rain throughout the land of Israel for three and a half years. What I find most remarkable was the confidence with which he made the declaration that shut the heavens. 1 Kings 17:1 says,

"And Elijah the Tishbite, of the inhabitants of Gilead, said to Ahab, "As the Lord God of Israel lives, before whom I stand, there shall not be dew nor rain these years, except at my word."

Can you imagine that? What gives a man such assurance as to make such a declaration? Knowing your place in God and your position as His representative on earth! Indeed, as we have seen before, according to Elijah's word, there was no rain throughout the specified period, until he had to pray again before the forces of nature (evaporation) and the forces of the atmosphere returned to normalcy and the heaven decided to open to send rain upon the earth. The implication is that if Elijah had died before the expiration of the three years within which he said there should be no rain, then the heaven would have remained locked for the Israelites for a long time.

What a challenge to you and to me, who have a greater

authority through the finished work of Jesus Christ on the cross! This is the time to arise and take our rightful place of dominion. We must possess all that God has bequeathed to us and be all that God has purposed us to be!

LAST NOTES

God is looking for men and women like Elijah, Joshua and other models of faith today. He is looking for believers who will use the power He has given to them to exercise dominion over the universe and dictate the course of events in their world. He is looking for those who can command the heavens, the earth and the seas, and make these forces bow to His purpose concerning their lives, their families, their churches, their communities and their nations.

God is counting on you and me to do this. I pray we do not fail Him. Enough of the enemies using our heritage to work against us! Enough of the heathen taking all the riches that belong to us. It is time for us to take our rightful position. It is time to take charge. It is time to rule YOUR world!